Licensed Insanities

Licensed Insanities

Religions and Belief in God in the Contemporary World

John Bowker

Darton, Longman and Todd
London

First published in 1987 by
Darton, Longman and Todd Ltd
89 Lillie Road, London SW6 1UD

ISBN 0 232 51725 8

British Library Cataloguing in Publication Data

Bowker, John
  Licensed insanities: religions and belief
  in God in the contemporary world
  1. God
  I. Title
  291.2′11   BL205

  ISBN 0–232–51725–8

Phototypeset by
Input Typesetting Ltd, London SW19 8DR
Printed and bound in Great Britain by
Anchor Brendon Ltd
Tiptree, Essex

Contents

For Margaret

Ultima talis erit, quae mea prima fides

Preface

This book is based on the Riddell Memorial Lectures given in the University of Newcastle in 1985. In the first lecture I faced the issue of whether there is any point retaining the study of religion in universities (or for that matter in education) at all. 'Faith', proposed H. L. Mencken, 'may be defined briefly as an illogical belief in the occurrence of the improbable.'[1] On what grounds can the study of such 'licensed insanities'[2] as religions be justified?

The case I argue is a pragmatic one. There are other arguments; but on that ground alone the case for religious studies is overwhelming. But the pragmatic case does not deal effectively with the fact that issues of truth are involved, particularly for theology. In the second lecture I took up the challenge to realistic language about God, put forward (to cite a recent example) by Don Cupitt's recent television series and book, *The Sea of Faith*. According to his own abrupt claim, 'Realism is dead';[3] we cannot talk realistically about unrealised and unrealisable non-entities of which, in his view, 'God' is an example. But is he right? People do, for example, pray to God as though to what is real and independent of themselves:

> Talk not to me of Summer Trees:
> The foliage of the mind
> A tabernacle is for Birds
> Of no corporeal kind
> And winds do go that way at noon

vii

To their Ethereal Homes
Whose bugles call the least of us
To undepicted Realms.[4]

But how can one possibly speak of undepicted realms? There is a familiar story which tells of a man who falls over the edge of a canyon – but by good fortune he grabs hold of a small bush as he starts to go down: so there he is, holding on, with the valley thousands of feet below him. 'Help!' he shouts. 'Is there anybody there?' To his amazement a voice answers, 'Yes, my son, what do you want?' 'Please,' he says, 'Get me back up the cliff – I'll do anything you say!' 'Anything?' And the man says desperately, 'Yes, anything.' And the voice says, 'Let go.' The man swallows hard, and then he says: 'Is there anybody else up there?' So the question, 'Is there anybody there?' was the question of the second lecture.

But the issue of whether one can or cannot talk realistically of God does not determine why people should wish to do so – or why people believe in God. Even if it is defensible to talk realistically of God, there are still many reasons why people do so (or why people believe in God) which do not require the existence of God. In the third lecture I looked at what some of those accounts are – accounts (which are strongly reductionist) which do not require the existence of God to account for belief in God. Do those reductionist accounts give an exhaustive or sufficient explanation of why belief in God occurs?

This book extends the lectures considerably, not only by incorporating comments and criticisms made at the time but also by amplifying the discussion and the examples. In no way could the lectures have been transformed into a book except for the extreme generosity of the university in making, and supplying to me, a transcript of the lectures as they were given. I am deeply grateful to the University of Newcastle, both for the original invitation and for the subsequent practical assistance.

My thanks are also due to John Polkinghorne for comment and advice on Chapter 2; to Catherine Walters for undertaking a substantial part of the final typing; and above all to Margaret, my wife, who through the traumas of a move to a new post refused to allow the impediments to academic work, which soon became apparent, to be as paralysing as they might have been. In a recent *Feminist Dictionary*, the entry under 'Acknowledgements' reads: 'Before feminism, that portion of a book where authors acknowledged the ideas and intellectual contributions of males, and the clerical and editorial assistance of females, and where men thanked their wives for critically reading their manuscripts without asking for coauthorship.'[5] But where thanks *are* due, and for a great deal more than that, what can I do but say thank you?

JB

Acknowledgements

The *Appendix: Religions as Systems* is reproduced from *Believing in the Church*, Report of the Doctrine Commission of the Church of England, by courtesy of SPCK.

The quotation from 'Soliloquy' is reprinted by permission of Faber and Faber Ltd from *The Collected Poems of Edwin Muir;* the quotation from 'Black Rook in Rainy Weather' is taken from *Collected Poems* by Sylvia Plath published by Faber and Faber Ltd © Ted Hughes 1981.

The Burning Fuse*

The Unacceptable Face of Religion

On Monday, 13 May 1985 the *Guardian* devoted page 3 to
'Overseas News'. There were twelve stories on the page, and
all but one were stories of violent behaviours or episodes: 'Sri
Lanka Killings "Revenge" '; 'Six Shot Dead in Bangladesh
Protests Over Koran Suit'; 'Cry Rings Out to Kill Extrem-
ists'; 'Death Toll of India Terror Bomb Reaches 80';
'Explosion in Teheran Kills 15'; and so on – and on: stories
like these are so familiar that we scarcely notice them. What
is not so familiar (or at least, not so often noticed) is how
frequently, in the most intransigent and apparently insoluble
of the disputes that lead to such violence, there are deep
religious involvements. Of the eleven stories of violence in the
Guardian that day, all but one had clear religious contributions
to them.

It was, I guess, for that reason that a correspondent wrote
to me (after a BBC programme on religions in the UK today)
describing religions as 'licensed insanities'. For in the
programme on which he was commenting (now the first
chapter in the book, *Worlds of Faith*) I had listed some of
the bitter conflicts or divisions which have strong religious
components in them:

> Bombs in Hyde Park and Ballykelly and many other parts
> of Northern Ireland, the destruction of Beirut, that whole
> conflict over Israel/Palestine and the Near East, the bitter
> divisions between black and white in the apartheid system
> of South Africa, Cyprus, India and Pakistan, Poland, the

---

* © 1986 *Zygon*. Part of this chapter appeared as 'Religion, War and Peace'
in *Zygon: Journal of Religion and Science*, December 1986.

Philippines, Iran, Afganistan, the list goes on and on. Even while we were making the first programme Sikhs were rioting in India, and in Northern Nigeria, 450 were killed in religious riots.[1]

All that was in 1983. None of those problems has disappeared; a few have been added. Religions are extremely dangerous animals; and one might well put up on their boundary the notice I saw once in a game reserve in Africa, 'Advance and be bitten'. And yet, despite the obvious involvement of religious beliefs and ideology in so many of the dangerous and destructive problems in the world, it is virtually impossible to find any politician or economist (let alone people who make the operative decisions in the worlds of commerce or industry) who has any serious knowledge of what religions are or why. As I put it in an article on this theme: 'One of the most obvious reasons why we seem to drift from one disastrous ineptitude to another is, ironically, that far too few politicians have read Religious Studies at a University. As a result, they literally *do not know* what they are talking about on almost any of the major international issues. They simply cannot.'[2]

It is, maybe, a symptom of this pragmatic contempt for religion that the very words 'theology' and 'religious' have become increasingly words of abuse. Norman St John Stevas was interviewed (June 1981) on a television programme in the series 'The Pursuit of Power', and he proclaimed very firmly, 'I am not a believer in the theology of monetarism': two days earlier Michael Shanks, as Chairman of the Consumers' Council, had declared of the gas and electricity industries: 'Pricing policy is not quite a scientific exercise, there's a bit of theology in it.' The thought that our gas bills are composed after a consultation with the Almighty may well explain why they are as they are, but I doubt if it is what Mr Shanks really had in mind. In its way it is merely a variation on the theme of 'how many Angels are there on the head of a pin?', another standard way of dismissing theology: 'They just spend their time discussing how many Angels there are on the head of a pin.' The fact that that discussion belonged far more profoundly – and crucially – to the history of mathematics is completely overlooked or ignored: so complex was the issue underlying that discussion

2

(concerning potential or actual infinities) that it was not until the end of the nineteenth century that it was resolved by Cantor in favour of actual infinities.[3]

And what about 'religiously'? That word too has begun to acquire a bad sense. In 1979 there was a disastrous fire in the Woolworths in Manchester. A company spokesman commented: 'There was no sprinkler system. That depends on a Local Authority's requirements and they do vary. We comply with them religiously, but in this case there was no such requirement.'[4] In the very same issue of the paper which contained that report there was an article on British car workers and the great shock they get when they go to Germany, because they find they have to clock-on at 7.12 a.m. exactly – the time being so precise, because the German unions have won an 18 minute breakfast break: 'As in all German companies the hours are rigorously, we might say almost religiously, applied by the management. Persistent late-comers face dismissal.'[5]

Perhaps this shift in language, whereby the terms 'theological' and 'religious' have acquired an edge of contempt or of scrupulosity, is not surprising. This age and generation has been declared to be the one that has 'come of age', and one in which we can achieve a 'religionless Christianity' – a further example of the word 'religion' acquiring a bad sense, since presumably whatever that is taken to be is regarded as an improvement on what went before.[6] Not that the belief that this generation has 'come of age' has to be equated with progress: 'Shall I tell you the signs of a New Age coming?' asked Stevie Smith:

> It is a sound of drubbing and sobbing
> Of people crying, We are old, we are old,
> And the sun going down and becoming cold.[7]

Nevertheless there has developed a sense that educated men and women must necessarily have grown out of religion, since it belongs to the infancy of the human race. Aldous Huxley put it elegantly (admittedly for an earlier generation):

> It is man's intelligence that makes him so often behave more stupidly than the beasts. An animal is without even the semblance of free will. Predestined by its instincts, it

has no choice. In every circumstance it must do the thing that the age-long experience of its species has found to be, on the whole, most profitable for specific survival. Judged by utilitarian standards, what it does is, generally, the right thing. (This applies, of course, only to the animal's behaviour in, statistically speaking, 'normal' circumstances. In circumstances that are to any considerable extent unlike average circumstances, the animal almost always does the hopelessly wrong thing.)

Man is so intelligent that he feels impelled to invent theories to account for what happens in the world. Unfortunately, he is not quite intelligent enough, in most cases, to find correct explanations. So that when he acts on his theories, he behaves very often like a lunatic. Thus, no animal is clever enough, when there is a drought, to imagine that the rain is being withheld by evil spirits, or as a punishment for its transgressions. Therefore you never see animals going through the absurd and often horrible fooleries of magic and religion. No horse, for example, would kill one of its foals in order to make the wind change its direction. Dogs do not ritually urinate in the hope of persuading heaven to do the same and send down rain. Asses do not bray a liturgy to cloudless skies. Nor do cats attempt, by abstinence from cat's meat, to wheedle the feline spirits into benevolence. Only man behaves with such gratuitous folly. It is the price he has to pay for being intelligent, but not, as yet, quite intelligent enough.[8]

For those who think of religion and theology in that way the educational point becomes obvious: why waste time, energy and scarce resources on religious studies and theology, when we know that neither has much to do with the real world – with the white heat of the scientific revolution in which Britain began to be forged on 1 October 1963?[9] Why waste time and money studying licensed insanities?

But then the point becomes obvious. Suppose we accept that definition, at least for the moment: the consequence would be, not to give up the study of religion: it would be the strongest possible argument for devoting far more time – and resources – to the attempt to understand such insanity a great deal more clearly than we do. Insanity, if it is unresearched and untreated, and if the reasons for it are unknown, can be a lethally dangerous phenomenon. What else can one do with it, until one understands what it is and why it occurs, except, as Dorothea Dix observed in Massachusetts in 1843, 'confine it in cages, closets, cellars, stalls and pens! Chained, naked, beaten with rods, and lashed into obedience'? As she went on to submit in a further Memorial to the Senate and House of Representatives in June 1848: 'I have myself seen more than nine thousand idiots, epileptics, and insane, in these United States ... bound with galling chains, bowed beneath fetters and heavy iron balls attached to drag chains, lacerated with ropes, scourged with rods.'[10]

That is certainly one way to treat religions. Various Communist regimes have been doing exactly that for more than forty years. But *are* religions as dangerous as I have been implying so far?

In one practical way they may be *more* dangerous, not less: consider how many of the nations or governments involved in the disputes alluded to on page 1 have, probably have, or state that they intend to have, nuclear weapons: it then becomes clear how much more likely it is that the second atomic/nuclear war will begin within the domain of the conflicts connected with religion, and not between Russia and America – though even in that most dangerous divide of all (bearing in mind on the one side Marx's views on religion and how it must wither away if the dictatorship of the proletariat is to be established, and on the other hand the religiously apocalyptic language with which some Americans describe Russia), it becomes clear that even in that divide there is a fundamental religious component.

The case therefore for reinforcing and strengthening the study of religion and religions is overwhelming. On pragmatic grounds alone we need to understand the dynamics of religious systems; we need to understand far more clearly than we do why religions in general matter so much to those who belong to them, why religious believers can be so passionate in their commitments, and why also religious believers are deeply, not to say violently, disturbed when their traditional belief patterns and practices are threatened or disturbed. Contrary to what Marx predicted (and contrary to what some western commentators seem to suppose),

5

religion is not withering away. It remains the context, or at least a part of the context, in which the majority of people alive on this planet today live their lives, or from which they derive important inspiration and judgment for their lives.

Religions as Resources for Life

That takes us at once to the part of the story missing so far. So far I have accepted – and emphasised – the extremely dangerous potentials within the religious domain; and in the final stages of this book there will be other examples (for example, the relish with which some religious believers engage in high-powered spiritual terrorisation). Too often religious education ignores or diminishes the unacceptable face of religion; whereas (since that unacceptable face is so obvious) it would, in my view, lead to far wiser insight if it began with (or at least included) Thomas Hardy's 'full look at the worst'.[11] But the plain fact remains that one reason why religions are so dangerous is because they are so important – and important to virtually every aspect of human life. Religions are, and remain, the resource and the inspiration of almost all the greatest achievements of human creativity, whether in art or architecture or agriculture, music, poetry, drama, spiritual exploration, even, in origin, the development of the natural sciences. This creative resourcefulness of religions remains as vital now as it has been in the past. In this very period, when we have been told that the sea of faith is going out, we have seen not only an immense numerical increase in some of the major religions but, even more to the point, we have seen very specific initiatives which have been derived not from a general goodwill but explicitly from Christian resources – such enterprises as the founding of the Little Brothers, the Hospice movement, L'Arche Communities, Christian Aid, Halfway Houses and the like. When Peter Benenson read in his morning paper, on the Underground, that two Portuguese students had been imprisoned for drinking a toast to freedom, his sense of horror drove him immediately to reflection in the church of St Martin-in-the-Fields; and from that reflection was born Amnesty International. In this respect, A. H. Clough in the nineteenth

6

century (who knew well at first hand the nature of doubt and scepticism) was a great deal more accurate than those in the twentieth century who see only a one-way flow, when he observed that if a tide goes out in some places it must no doubt find a level somewhere else:

> For while the tired waves, vainly breaking,
>   Seem here no painful inch to gain,
> Far back, through creeks, and inlets making,
>   Comes silent, flooding in, the main.[12]

And since that *is* the verse of a poem, it is a point of the same kind to recognise that in this very same period, of the last 100 years, we have been living through one of the greatest ages of Christian poetry that has yet occurred.

So religions are not unequivocally and exclusively bad news. The paradox to be grasped is that religions are highly dangerous *because they are so important* and because they create so much in, and of, human life. But *why* are they so important? Not simply, one would suppose, in order to help us write more beautiful poetry or design more marvellous buildings. The really fundamental reason is that religions are a consequence of extremely ancient and long-running explorations by the human animal of its own nature and its possibilities, *and* of how best it can sustain the possibilities of its own continuing life. Religions are the oldest (and therefore by evolutionary definition the most successful) 'cultural packages' which have protected and enhanced the replication of genes and the nurture of children. That kind of observation, derived as it is from sociobiology, may seem suspect, since sociobiology is itself very controversial – so it is in any case an issue to be taken up further (pp. 88ff). But the basic observation is not in itself controversial: religions (whatever else they may be) are at least highly successful cultural creations, through which human beings have secured and enhanced the probability of gene replication and the successful nurture of children. Furthermore they are (to pick up the vital observation of the American psychologist Donald Campbell) extremely well-winnowed through time. They have been tested and sifted for effectiveness through time and in experience.

So religions are a consequence of explorations – explorations of what this strange architecture of atoms and molecules (which constitutes you or me or any other human being) really is capable of being or of becoming – what *are* the possibilities which are open to it? – and also they represent social achievements of stability and protection, of both genetic and cultural information. And from the point of view of our own participation in those achievements, it is important to remember how stable the genome (genetic material) is, so that what it produces in the past is by no means inaccessible to us by way of understanding.

These points may seem dense and obscure if they are unfamiliar – and they will be discussed in more detail when we come, later on, to consider why people believe in God. At this point, it is enough to notice how vital religions have been for human survival *and* for cultural and individual discoveries. It means that religions are just as much a consequence of human curiosity as are biology, physics or the study of Greek antiquity. The difference from those other explorations is that religions are a consequence of explorations of an idiosyncratic, *sui generis*, subject matter, an exploration of what we are capable of allowing the available human energy to become at the furthest stretch of its possibility. It is of that inner exploration that Thoreau was writing at the end of his book *Walden:*

> Is it the source of the Nile, or the Niger, or the Mississippi or a North West Passage around this continent, that we would find? Are these the problems which most concern mankind? Be rather the Mungo Park, the Lewis and Clarke and Frobisher of your own streams and oceans . . . Nay, be a Columbus to whole new continents and worlds within you, opening new channels, not of trade, but of thought.[13]

Then Thoreau went on to warn us: 'It is easier to sail many thousands of miles through cold and storm and cannibals in a government ship with 500 men and boys to assist one, than it is to explore the private sea, the Atlantic and the Pacific Ocean of one's own being alone.'[14]

But in making that addition Thoreau, while he was certainly being honest to his time of solitude in Walden Wood, nevertheless was completely missing the reason why religions exist. The basic reason why religions exist, is that we *never* have to make those explorations of our own nature and possibility alone. In fact we cannot do so, because we would have to invent and discover everything for ourselves. In that case life in each generation would have to begin *de novo:* each of us would have to invent the wheel and discover fire all over again. The point is obvious but it is, all the same, important. The point is that information does not float around the universe at random: information to *be* information has to be coded, channelled, protected and received. Between humans it can then be shared and transmitted from one life, or from one generation, to another. And since information can also be stored, it is for all these reasons that John of Salisbury could report (in a quotation much appreciated by Isaac Newton): 'Bernard of Chartres used to say that we, like dwarfs on the shoulders of giants, can see more and farther, not because we are keener and taller, but because of the greatness by which we are carried and exalted.'[15]

But that kind of 'circus-acrobat construction' cannot happen randomly or by chance. Wherever human communities have made what they believe to be important or precious discoveries, they have devised (or they have allowed to come into being) the organised means of their protection and transmission, and thus they make sure that those discoveries are transmitted into other lives and other generations beyond their own. Equally (and this is just the other side of the coin) where some item of *gnosis* (of knowledge or information) is so important for survival or success (or at least in so far as it is believed to be so), then of course communities have often gone to the other extreme: they have organised the protection and transmission of information so well that the outsider cannot gain access to it. There are industrial secrets as well as military secrets, and often there are religious secrets.

Religions as Systems

So, whatever else religions may be, at the very least they are systems organised for the process, protection and transmission of information. That is why there are mystery religions and missionary religions. Mystery religions are those which protect the transmission of vital saving knowledge so securely that only the initiates can gain access to it.[16] Missionary religions are equally well organised but in such a way that the transfer of information is on open offer. Either way round, introverted or extroverted, the really essential point is that there will be no religions at all if there are not individuals within them who believe that the information which they have received and which is incorporated in their own lives (literally embodied in such a way that it informs and forms in themselves) is so important that it really must be preserved, protected and transmitted. Consequently religions are organised for the process and transmission of information – of Dharma in Hinduism, of *ariya-atthangika-magga* (the Noble Eightfold Path) in Buddhism, the conditions of *berith* (of covenant) in Judaism, of *sharia*ᶜ (the consequence of Qur'an and *hadith*) in Islam; and so on.

Religions are then organised in immensely different ways for the transmission of information. Systems, including religious systems, can be very diverse. One of the few things they have in common is an emphasis on how important women have been in the process – a point strongly emphasised by those interviewed in *Worlds of Faith:* 'Women', says Mrs Pancholi (to quote but one example), 'are the transmitters of culture in Hindu tradition, and this role lies in the hands of women. I don't think a man has time or even the patience to do that.'[17] Therefore she was able to go on to argue that in Hindu perception women are actually much more important than the men, who (poor dumb creatures) are not much good for anything except going out to work.

If, then, we are to understand why adherents to religions are often so passionate and violent, we need first to understand the extent to which religions are *systems*, and why. On religions as systems, I have written at length elsewhere,[18] and my attempt to summarise what is involved in this is reprinted in the Appendix. But briefly, systems are the organised ways in which otherwise disparate and unrelated parts are linked to some common purpose or enterprise. 'Trade unions, political parties, professional football, Marks and Spencer's, the Royal Airforce, British Leyland, the United Nations, . . . have to be *systematically* ordered if continuity is to be assured (or at least attempted), and if decisions affecting the organisation are to be made and implemented; and there are effective and ineffective ways of achieving this.'[19]

An important implication of this is that systems, including religious systems, require boundaries in order to maintain their identity, and in order to assure the protection and transmission of information. Those boundaries may be metaphorical (the body of Christ), or they may be literal (thus, until recently an orthodox brahmin was not supposed to travel outside the boundary of India, nor even, ideally, outside the boundary of his province). So if we ask the further question, '*Why* are religions necessarily systems?' a key point lies in the importance of the information which religious systems are protecting and making available for appropriation into life. It is so important, extensive and diverse that it *requires* elaborate systems to protect it. Information, particularly in the religious case, is very far from being simply words, whether written, spoken or sung. Much more is involved than the transfer of verbal items. What are being transmitted are such things as style, method, wisdom, insight, technique, behaviour; and a great deal of all that is transmitted in the religious case by entirely non-verbal means, by action, liturgy, silence, ritual, dance, decoration, and so on. But in all this, the fundamental and essential point is this: for those involved in the process, the religious information may be far more important than any other information for which we organise the systematic means of transmission. The information which religions are transmitting is frequently believed by those who are living it, and therefore transmitting it, to be a great deal more important in the long run (and often in the short run) than physics or biology or history, or any of those other systematised transmissions of information, which usually have a higher priority in university budgets.

The reason is obvious: religion has to do, not just with the organisation of life day by day, week by week, year by year; it has to do also with what you or I, the human organisation of energy, may immediately become in the transformation of life and its judgments, and may ultimately also become in terms of salvation, nirvana, *moksha*, union with God, or whatever else may be held out as an ultimate goal or concern. It may be the case that the religions are entirely wrong, or even just partly wrong, about what they believe to be the ultimate case; but that does not affect the point. The point is that what are on offer in religious traditions are both the goals to

11

which any humans may reasonably and hopefully aspire, and also the resources to help them to make the journey.

Not all these goals are ultimate (in the sense that they lie beyond death). By far the majority are immediate, within the boundary of this life. And although religions may now point to goals that lie beyond death (such things as salvation, paradise, *moksha*, nirvana), *in origin* all the major continuing religious traditions, both East and West, were based on a 'this life', 'this worldly' experience (particularly experience of what is called, in English, God), *not* on a belief that there was going to be something worthwhile after death. It is the exact opposite of what Marx and Freud supposed. In all the major long-standing religions there was no belief *originally* that there would be a conscious continuity of life with God beyond death. This is probably most familiar in the case of the Jews. Almost the whole of Tanach (of what Christians refer to as the Old Testament) was written without any belief that there would be a worthwhile life with God after death. In other words, contrary to what Marx and Freud and many others have said (that religions came into being in order to offer compensation in heaven for all the ills and evils of this life) in fact, in origin, the major continuing religious traditions came into being without any belief that there will be any kind of worthwhile life beyond the grave.[20]

So, fundamentally, religions are a consequence of *this*-life, *this*-worldly discoveries, whatever further inferences may subsequently have been drawn. This means that quite apart from any belief in what may or may not happen after death, religions are the basic systemic means through which individuals and communities have organised and protected their own continuity and survival, and have identified the worth and value of being human. Religions are the basic and primordial cultural achievements, through which gene replication is secured, enhanced and protected. *But also* religions have been validated to their adherents and participants, not simply because they create stable contexts for breeding and nurture, but because they have in any case identified (and continued to make available to others in later generations) particular achievements and opportunities in the exercise of this particular human energy. It is this quality of discovery and achievement in the religious case which means that no matter how important physics or history or any other subject in the curriculum may be (and obviously they *are* important – which is why the human community has organised systematic ways of transmitting those traditions, in schools, colleges and universities), they are nothing like as important potentially, for many people, as the information which is protected and transmitted in the religious systems. For these systems contain those traditional and long-established wisdoms, which led Campbell to observe that they are indeed 'well winnowed'. Religions are a consequence of successive generations testing, correcting, confirming, extending, changing, the accumulating wisdoms of experience.

None of this is unfamiliar. In a different way this is exactly what the sciences are, and how they proceed. They too are well-winnowed traditions, tested, corrected, confirmed and extended through the process of time. They are well-winnowed traditions, in which increasing reliability is achieved, and in which the false or the ineffective or the illusory is winnowed out. Of course the history of science is not as simple as that;[21] but the general point remains clear: the sciences do correct and change themselves through the course of time, and require systematic means in order to do so. But so too do religions: religions also are well-winnowed traditions, and they do as a matter of fact correct and change themselves;[22] and they too have to be organised as systems for this process, of appropriation from the past, embodiment in the present and extension into the future (other lives and subsequent generations) to take place. However, that means, as we have just seen, that they require boundaries; and it is here that the tensions begin: religions are so ancient and so well winnowed through time that they are, generally speaking, extremely reluctant to change. The reluctance becomes even more acute when religions appeal to revelation; but even without revelation, religions are predictably always going to be conservative, simply because people within them believe there are important things to conserve: the information they are processing is believed by many of those involved (and they are often the operators of the systems) to be so vital that they are bound to be reluctant to change, or even, frequently, to adapt. In their own perception they must defend and preserve what has been transmitted to them, which has given identifiable value and significance (or, to use religious language, salvation or enlightenment) to their lives.

So the more a religious system is threatened, whether by persecution or by the proximity of a rival system, or even by a drift into secular indifference, the more likely it is that at least some people in that system will begin to monitor and maintain the boundaries of the system with much more careful attention to the past and to detail. That is to say, they attend to the fundamentals which have given rise to that tradition and which have been maintaining and sustaining it. Not surprisingly therefore at the present time we find so many variations on the theme of fundamentalism in all religions – an insistence on the fundamental conditions which are believed to guarantee the continuity and the achievement of what has been on offer so far in that system. It may sound very complicated, but it simply means that the theme of conservative fundamentalism will occur in all religions, not just in Iran or the Vatican or Pakistan or the Sudan or the southern states of America; and those (and other) variations on a theme will occur because of what is required of systems to be effective *as* systems for the protection and the process of information.

It means also that the operators of religious systems (such people as popes, imams, rabbis, pandits) are likely to remain boundary-minded, as indeed are many of those who belong to religious systems. There will be, at the least, a sensitivity concerning the protection and transmission of information (which, after all, has been by definition important to themselves) into other lives and other generations beyond their own. Under threat, more bluntly, there will be a determination to maintain the system and its boundaries. And where there are boundaries, even metaphorical boundaries, there will always be what we may well call 'border incidents'. That is why it is easy to take a world map, draw on it the boundaries where religious systems or subsystems are adjacent to each other, and see, not only that these boundaries identify existing trouble-spots, but also that they enable prediction of where new incidents or episodes of conflict are likely to occur.

Religions, Warfare and Violence

Is all this far too pessimistic? Certainly it is one-sided. Of course, on the other side, we have to keep in mind that brief allusion, made earlier, to the fact that religions are the resource of virtually all the greatest achievements of human creativity and exploration – quite apart from their paramount adaptive contribution to human evolution and survival. All that alone would be more than enough to justify their place in any worthwhile education. But we are looking at a more pragmatic and elementary point, that we *must* understand the dynamics of religious systems much more clearly than we do, if we are to have any hope of unravelling those complex problems which bring so much misery and destruction to so many people. I am not in any way suggesting that religions alone *cause* those problems. Certainly not. There are constraints derived from geography, economics, history and no doubt human malevolence and wickedness. But religions (that is, constraints derived from religious ideation and the necessities inherent in the nature of systems) are undoubtedly powerful within the total network of constraints which control these destructive events into their happening.

Not least is that so because all religions will justify violence in certain circumstances (the nature of the circumstances being differently identified in different religions). This is true even of religions which have a reputation for being tolerant, such as Hinduism or Buddhism, with its strong commitment to *ahimsa*, non-violence. The point was put succinctly by a commentator on the recent outbreak of violence between the Sinhalese and the Tamils in Sri Lanka – the Sinhalese being mainly Buddhist, the Tamils mainly Hindu: asked what the chances of reconciliation are, he replied, 'You will never achieve peace in Sri Lanka, until you throw away the Mahavamsa.'

The point of that comment is that the Mahavamsa, the Great Chronicle, is the early epic history of Sri Lanka, recording, among other things, how the island was visited by the Buddha and became Buddhist. It includes episodes in which Buddhist kings went to war with the blessing and support of Buddhist monks (the *sangha*), not least against the Damilas. Thus when King Dutthagamani (c. 101–77 BCE)

15

decided to expand his territory in Sri Lanka and attack the Damilas, he appealed to the *sangha* in these terms: 'I will go on to the land on the further side of the river to bring glory to the doctrine [*dhamma*]. Give us, that we may treat them with honour, bhikkhus [monks] who shall go on with us, since the sight of bhikkhus is blessing and protection for us' (*Mahavamsa*, xxv.3).

Having won his victory over all thirty-two of the Damila kings, Dutthagamani established a single kingdom in the whole island. But then he began to have second thoughts about the millions he had killed in his wars. Immediately the *arahants* (those who have attained the goal of Buddhism and have true insight) sent eight of their number to reassure the king – and they did so on two grounds: first that he had actually only killed one and a half people, since the rest were in effect not truly human; and second that in any case the evaluation of deeds rests on the state of mind or attitude in which they are performed – and the king had specifically acted to bring glory to Buddhism. They said:

> From this deed arises no hindrance in your way to heaven. Only one and a half human beings have been slain here by you, O lord of men. The one had come into the (three) refuges, the other had taken on himself the five precepts.[23] Unbelievers and men of evil life were the rest, not more to be esteemed than beasts. But as for you, you will bring glory to the doctrine of the Buddha in manifold ways; therefore cast away care from your heart, O ruler of men! Thus exhorted by them the great king took comfort. . . . Should a man think on the hosts of human beings murdered for greed in countless myriads, and should he carefully keep in mind the evil (arising from that), and should he also very carefully keep in mind mortality as being the murderer of all, then will he, in this way, shortly win freedom from suffering and a happy condition. (*Mahavamsa*, xxv, 101–end)

These points are made, not in order to take sides in that dispute, still less to express antagonism against Buddhists or Hindus, but only to illustrate the fact that all religions, at some point and in different ways, will justify war or violence, even if only as the lesser of two evils. What we have in this instance is not a Thirty Years War of religion, but a two thousand and thirty years war of religion; and the extent to which some Sinhalese still see the matter as one of defending Sinhala Buddhist culture has been well-documented in such works as *Sri Lanka: Racism and the Authoritarian State*.[24] Gandhi emphasised the priority of non-violence in his interpretation of the Hindu tradition. But the Bhagavadgita, a deeply fundamental text for virtually all Hindus, tells Arjuna that he *must* fight and kill his kinsmen, because it is his *dharma* (his appropriate behaviour) as a warrior to do so; and because also, in Hinduism, it is only possible to kill the superficial, outward appearance of something, never the abiding, enduring reality which underlies all appearance. And Gandhi was assassinated by two orthodox Hindus who believed it was their own *dharma* to act against his misappropriation of tradition (though more immediately, of its finances).

This acceptance of warfare and violence in some circumstances (in the western religions the Holy War, the Just War and *jihad*) means that religions are realistic about evil, and about its intention and capacity to destroy. This realism even goes so far as to accept that the forces of chaos, evil and destruction may prevail – not ultimately, but immediately; all religions live with apocalyptic scenarios of an End to the prevailing order, in chaos or violence or terror. So much is this so, that largely thanks to religion, the very word 'apocalypse', which in Greek meant originally 'the uncovering of the head', or 'the making manifest of the unknown' (hence seeing into the future, both of good and evil), has come to have a negative sense. It is now virtually a synonym for 'cataclysmic destruction', as in the title of the film, *Apocalypse Now*.

It follows that religions are not necessarily dismayed by the possible destruction of the world. They may indeed regard such cataclysmic events as, say, a local nuclear conflict as 'signs of the end', vindications of their own beliefs. Even more alarming (for those who do not share those apocalyptic beliefs), some believers may feel an obligation on themselves to promote the very circumstance itself. At the least, it is not aberrant for such people to look for signs that the cookie has begun to crumble. Buddhists believe that we are living in the *meppo*, Hindus that we are living in the *kali yuga* (both of them being views, within a cyclical understanding of time, that we are living near the end of the cycle when evil and destruction will prevail), Christian Adventists look for the Second Coming, and ponder the Four Horsemen of the Apocalypse, Lubavitch Hasidic Jews chant on the streets of New York, 'We want the Messiah, and we want him now.'

These may be minority voices. But they illustrate an acceptance of warfare and violence, which reinforces the predictable inclination of many people, in strong systems, to defend the boundaries of those systems when they seem to be coming under threat. Of course there is much more to be said about religions than this. There are many counteravailing voices and actions which point in different directions. On that same page of the *Guardian* which reported so many stories of violence with religious components in them, in the bottom left hand corner was an advertisement for the Society of Friends, which offered a free copy of *Introducing Quakers*. But it was nevertheless a minute proportion of the page.

If less has been said so far about the resources within the religious traditions which require an attempt at reconciliation and peace, it is because I have been trying, as directly and briefly as possible, to indicate why religions matter to those who belong to them, why religions are bound to be conservative (especially if they find themselves in a minority or under stress), why therefore religious believers do tend to become very passionate about the defence of tradition and their system, and why consequently it is absolutely essential and urgent for us to understand the nature and the dynamics of these systems: because they are not going to go away, they are not going to give way to each other and they are not going to merge into a single world religion. There have indeed been attempts to establish unifying world religions, but so far each of them has ended up as another religion (that is, another separate system). Islam, for example, began as a claim that since there can be only one God, there can only be one single *'umma* (human community of faith) deriving its life from God and returning its life to him. Bahais emerged in the nineteenth century from the context of Islam, proclaiming the essential unity of all religions. Yet both became separated systems; and some Muslims in Iran now persecute Bahais with great ferocity.

The Differences between Religions

'What, then, is to be done?' as Prince Oblonsky asked, sitting on the edge of his sofa, on the morning after his wife had discovered that he has been unfaithful with the young French governess.[25] What can we do to help or encourage these strong systems to find ways of coexisting with others, particularly where the overlap of boundaries has already led to 'border incidents' – or to outright war? One common procedure is to draw religions together in order to identify those beliefs and objectives which they have in common, and in order to mobilise their support against a common enemy. 'The question that arises, and may have to be debated', according to A. K. Brohi, an attorney and former cabinet minister in Pakistan, is this:

> What is it that has overtaken those who subscribe to the three Abrahamic religions [Judaism, Christianity and Islam] that they cannot stand shoulder to shoulder to face the assault that the Antichrist is making upon the lives of a vast section of mankind? How is it that the followers of these three religions do not take a united stand against the forces of Atheism, materialism and historicism in terms of which *communist doctrine* is penetrating in a large way into the soul-life of the teeming millions of the world?[26]

But the paradox of this approach (seeking the common ground between religions) is that it is too easy to achieve. In making the programmes, *Worlds of Faith*, I asked people to summarise what they believed to be the essential point and quality of their own religion. The answers, listed out of context, might apply to *any* of the religions – and out of context, it is not always easy to identify which of the religions is being summarised:

(*a*) My main aim of this life is to lead a peaceful and helpful life, and to serve humanity in any way I can, and not to be a hindrance to anyone. That is the aim of my life, and I try my utmost to achieve this aim.

(*b*) Peace and harmony and tolerance and compassion and generosity: I think these are the things; and I think these are very, very important – and honesty: honesty for yourself

19

and for others, without any discrimination, without colour or creed. And compassion has to extend not only to human beings, but beyond all human beings to all creatures.

(c) I wouldn't have said this a few years ago, but I think I'll say it now, that if you reduce the whole of it, as they say, to a few words, it's, Love thy neighbour as thyself. That incorporates and takes in the real ethic.

(d) I would say that the real characteristics are accepting things, and giving, caring, loving, about everyone, not just about your own family: I think it must include everyone that you come in contact with, that you must care – always to care, that's the important thing.

(e) Without my religion, my belief, my faith, I wouldn't be a human being at all: I would be just as useless as a weed in a garden. It's my belief that keeps me up. I walk in the street sometimes, and many people look at me and say a lot of things which they shouldn't say, but I forget all about it, because my religion says, Tolerance, patience, obedience. I take every other fellow as a human being. So my religion is important to me. It is because of my religion that I survive.[27]

So it is not difficult to get religious leaders to agree on large, general issues of goodwill and morality; and there may well be some preliminary virtue in helping religious people to see how much they *do* in fact agree on. But it carries us very little further in resolving practical issues unless we recognise how profoundly different in practice the religions may be in the ways in which they move towards a superficially common objective.

To take an example: most parents in any religion (and their religious leaders) would probably agree that they do not want their daughters, while still at school, to become pregnant or addicted to drugs. That is a perfectly sensible, general goal, and there would be no problem in getting a statement from all religions agreeing that this is desirable. Therefore we might conclude that all religions are really different routes (different roads) to the same goal. But in fact the roads by which religions move really are *different:* and it is in the detail that the religions become radically incompatible with each other and often with a secular society. If we take further the example of protecting one's daughters: in some religions this goes right down into the detail of deportment, clothes, behaviour, who they may have as friends, when and to what time they can be out in the evening, whether they can be educated with boys, and whether they should initiate the quest for a marriage partner. For the parents concerned, this is not a matter of persuasion and trust, or of initiating their daughters into their own independence of choice and responsibility: it is, for the parents, a matter of obligation and of *their own* responsibility, because they are accountable, within the terms of their own religious system, for how the children entrusted to them are looked after; and the account will have to be rendered through, for example, *samsara* (the round of re-birth) or, in the case of Muslims, on the *yaum udDin*, the day of Judgment: 'Each one of us is a caretaker [*ra'iy*]', said Muhammad, 'and is responsible for those under his care.'

Religions may seem superficially to be similar, but in fact they are radically different: the differences go to the *radix*, the root of behaviour. That is so, because each religion carries with it its own implicit anthropology – that is, its own account of what human nature *is*. Thus, the mention of *samsara* in the previous paragraph is a reminder of the Hindu belief that human nature is constituted in such a way that the Self underlying my appearance (the essential, undying, enduring reality which underlies my, and every other, appearance) will be reborn repeatedly, until I attain *moksha*, or release; and 'repeatedly' may mean as many as 84 million times. Buddhists agree that there will be long sequences of connected reappearance, but they do not believe that there is any abiding, substantial 'self' being reborn – there are only the long sequences of continuing, caused and effected, reappearance. These are different anthropologies from each other, and both of them are different from the anthropologies of the western religions.

Or to take another example: kamikaze pilots or Buddhist Viet-cong guerillas or Shiite Muslims driving lorries as bombs, all believe that there are more important things in life than living: the way in which they die has direct consequences for what they will be after death. Yet they hold that belief for different reasons. They are different anthropologies from each other and from other religions.

21

Again (as another example), the status of women in (most) religions seems to many, looking in from the outside, to be humiliating and repressive – not least because the operators of religious systems are usually men:

> Patriarchy is itself the prevailing religion of the entire planet, and its essential message is necrophilia. All of the so-called religions legitimating patriarchy are mere sects subsumed under its vast umbrella/canopy. They are essentially similar, despite the variations. All – from buddhism and hinduism to islam, judaism, christianity, to secular derivatives such as freudianism, jungianism, marxism, and maoism – are infrastructures of the edifice of patriarchy. All are erected as parts of the male's shelter against anomie. And the symbolic message of all the sects of the religion which is patriarchy is this: Women are the dreaded anomie. Consequently, women are the objects of male terror, the projected personifications of 'the Enemy', the real objects under attack in all the wars of patriarchy.[28]

The case may seem overstated – until one reflects *inter multa alia* on the extraordinary contortions of Christians resisting the ordination of women. *Nevertheless* it is frequently the women involved who resist most emphatically the intrusion of outsiders (whose judgments are made from their own circumstantial anthropologies) disrupting a life-way which the women themselves want and desire (see p. 10). They are living with different anthropologies.[29]

It then happens that people carry from their different religious anthropologies very different attitudes to illness, authority, work, school, family, the outsider, those in need, and so on. Do those differences make any difference? Clearly they do, if they create different identifications of value or of obligation. To take a very direct and simple illustration of this: some years ago a documentary was shown on British television of a return visit to the so-called 'death railway', constructed by prisoners-of-war under the supervision of Japanese guards. Part of the line has remained open, and at the end of the line there is now a flourishing plantation carved out of the jungle – a plantation which obviously could not have been brought into existence but for the railway. The interviewer asked the owner whether he had any uneasy feelings about his own prosperity having been built on so many deaths. He replied that of course he was sorry that it had happened, but that life comes and goes – and anyway, he asked (turning on the interviewer), why do you put such a value on the individual appearance on this earth? The different anthropology issues in very different actions. In the Japanese case there existed a distinctive sense of the close connection between the spirits of the dead and the soil of Japan, and also between the living and the spirit of their ancestors; and to die well or obediently in war makes a return to Japan a great deal more certain than annual leave. This is so deep that even the arrival of Buddhist missionaries in Japan, who introduced to the Japanese for the first time promises of heaven and threats of hell-fire in domains far removed from Japan, failed to dislodge the indigenous Japanese belief. Kunio Yanagida has summarised this very clearly:

> We do not know how old this belief in the ancestral spirit remaining on this land of ours to protect their posterity and make them prosper may be. But it is important to note that the cosmopolitan idea of Buddhism, which preached that the departed soul would leave this land to go to some faraway place which did not belong within any national boundary, was very strange to the Japanese people. Surrounded by nations who believed the other world to be far away and cut off from them, and in spite of long years of Buddhist influence, the Japanese alone retained their belief in the closeness and accessibility of the departed spirits of their ancestors.[30]

Those beliefs, arising from a different anthropology, helped to create a powerful justification for actions and attitudes in war which to other belief-systems seemed incomprehensible, or worse. When the International Military Tribunal was set up in 1946 it classified war crimes in three categories: crimes against peace, conventional war crimes, and crimes against humanity. Crimes against humanity seemed self-evidently to be crimes of atrocity. Yet the actual word 'humanity' (as in 'human rights') begs the very question at issue: an atrocity in one anthropology is not necessarily so in another; and of the 1,068 Japanese prisoners who were executed (or who died in prison), it is clear that the majority remained committed to the view that their actions in the war were justified. Seven hundred and one of those who died as war criminals left some kind of personal statement. The statements were collected and published under the title *Seiko no Isho*. Kazuko Tsurumi analysed the statements, and showed that 87.4 per cent of those condemned refused to accept any kind of guilt, except that they had failed the emperor and their fellow countrymen, which was indeed Hideki Tojo's own attitude: 'As a man responsible for the waging of the war, I deeply regret that the war ended with our defeat . . . I deeply regret what I have done and apologise to the Emperor and to my countrymen.' Of those who refused to accept guilt, 30 per cent specifically expressed a belief that their spirits would return to protect their families and their fatherland, and for that reason they were able to approach their own death undisturbed.[31]

The purpose of quoting that example is not to make some value-judgment, for or against. It is to emphasise that differences between religions may – and frequently in practice do – make a difference.[32] Some parts of what religions claim to be the case are logically incompatible with each other: the religions may all be wrong, but they cannot all be right – not in everything that they claim to be the case. So how can they live or coexist with each other? To take a particular example, how can they coexist in the United Kingdom, which is now religiously plural in an obvious way, and in which already we know that some Roman Catholics and some Protestants *cannot* coexist peacefully (albeit in a very special circumstance in Northern Ireland)?

The Coexistence of Religions

The immediate problem in this country is one of geography. The geography of religious space is inevitably important, given that systems have to be systems in order to function effectively for the protection and transmission of information. Systems as complex as religions require literal as well as metaphorical space. How do we handle the religious imperative for space in the United Kingdom, which is the size of a medium-size American state? It is roughly the size of

24

Wyoming; and about one third of the United Kingdom, in the north of Scotland, is sparsely inhabited in any case. Religions coexist in India or in the United States but there is considerably more space in those countries for distribution. But is such distribution desirable, given the consequences of cultural ghettos, the caste system and the pressure for degrees of autonomy among, for example, Sikhs in the Punjab? Or is some kind of autonomy precisely the goal to be aimed for? What should be done in practice to give space for the continuity, development and identity of these distinct cultural and religious traditions?

That last question immediately gives rise, for some people, to another set of questions: should we do anything? Why should we make provision for religious pluralism? What is the basis for it? The most obvious answer lies in a regard for Article 18 of the United Nations Universal Declaration of Human Rights: 'Everyone has the right to freedom of thought, conscience and religion; this right includes freedom to change his religion or belief, and freedom, either alone or in community with others and in public or private, to manifest his religion or belief in teaching, practice, worship and observance.'

But in practice the foundation and basis for coexistence, toleration and freedom of belief, are extremely different in different cultures and traditions. In America, reflecting the European experience, Church and State were deliberately separated from each other. In India a participant diversity can, within limits, be tolerated because in the Indian anthropology (since we are going to be reborn 84 million times) sooner or later we may have to participate in *all* the religions. There are many different paths to the same goal. In this country the Toleration Act of 1689 was a completely different enterprise. It was based on the premise of something like a National Church: the Earl of Nottingham introduced, not one but two bills, the first for comprehension, offering generous terms on which dissenters might be admitted to the Church of England, the second, the Toleration Act, to deal with the few who would not allow themselves to be so comprehended. It was only when King William appeared in the House of Lords to propose the abolition of the Test and Corporation Acts that fears overflowed and the Comprehension Bill was lost. The Toleration Act went through on its own, addressed to a different and much larger constituency. All that is very different from a Bill of Rights, and clearly a very odd basis for a secular toleration now. So, on what basis in this country *should* the toleration of conscience and belief rest? Should we extend toleration to religions which themselves are deliberately separatist and divisive, or to religions which, if they were in control, would certainly not extend a comparable toleration in reverse? It is much easier to build a mosque in Regent's Park than to build a cathedral in Medina. Obviously a Muslim would say that Regent's Park is not as important to a Christian as Medina is to a Muslim, and that is true. But in general, is the extension of toleration reciprocal? Or, to apply the point differently, should all new religions and cults be equally tolerated? The Cotterell proposals in the European parliament clearly felt that *some* religions should carry a warning on the package, that they are dangerous to spiritual health. But *are* they? And who decides? And are the Moonies a charity – to keep the questions in the immediate and practical domain?

All these issues, which have been in the headlines in recent years, lead to a third set of questions – or perhaps more accurately to a clear parting of the ways, where we will have to make a decision of principle and policy: granted that freedom of conscience and belief is still secure in this country, what should we actually do to implement it? The options here are very serious. It is decisively important, as we have seen, for religions to feel that the continuity of their own tradition is secure and that the transmission is protected. What should those outside a particular tradition do? Should we try to reinforce that stability, which arises from security, by encouraging and allowing separate identity (and here the issue of separate schools is inescapable)? Or should we try to guarantee the very principle of toleration itself by encouraging as much integration as possible, above all in the schools, by bringing people together into friendship and respect for each other? Given the long battles to achieve the liberties of this country, it is still (thankfully) highly likely that we will favour the second option, the route of integration. But that route, by encouraging assimilation, is precisely the one which is very threatening to some religious systems because they believe they require distance and separation in order to secure the continuity of their own tradition. There was a brief example of this in the last election, in a television discussion in Birmingham before an invited audience. The then Chairman of the Conservative Party, Cecil Parkinson, tried to defend the famous or infamous Conservative poster, which displayed a black face and said of Labour, 'They call you Black but we call you British'. In the agitation of the discussion Mr Parkinson continued to take, in an increasingly bewildered way, what he believed to be the liberal and integrating line, until a young woman in the audience jumped up and shouted, 'Can't you understand that we want to be Black *and* British?'

But what does it *mean* to be both x and y; or a or b or c, and y? Should we expect and encourage the sacrifice of sheep, as happened recently in a London street, to inaugurate Ramadan? Or polygamy? Or separate state schools for each religion that can demonstrate a majority in the local population (since we already have schools for Jews and Christians, and even for Christians in different subsystems of the whole)? Of course the questions are extreme. But they are intended to emphasise that for some of these strong systems, what is important is not a particular issue, but the defence and preservation of a whole life-way, which has been inherited from the past, and which must be maintained. This too was put strongly by a Muslim in a television debate, when a headmaster pointed out how, in his school (on the premise of toleration), the school assembly was converted into a form of the great Muslim festivals, 'Id alFitr and 'Id alDua', when they occur. In an almost angry contempt the Muslim replied that that was futile in relation to the experience of being Muslim and growing up as a Muslim child.

'What, then, is to be done?' to repeat the question. First and most urgently we need to understand, much more clearly and accurately than we do, what actually *is* required within each system for its maintenance and continuity (on the assumption, made earlier, that they are not going to disappear and that they are not going to be banned by legislation). What is required is a much more detailed and serious analysis of what the necessary conditions for continuity in each religious system really are. We need to know what really is, as well as what is perceived to be, indispensable and necessary

27

for each religious system to continue and to transmit what it regards as its wisdom and practice into another generation.

Clearly people in each religious system (and certainly operators of such systems) think they know what those conditions are: if they are asked, in the abstract, to specify the necessary conditions for their survival, then the answer will be an extremely long list. It will include virtually every mark of identity in the system – so the turban of the Sikhs will be added to the Five Ks[33] as though it is a sixth. Yet in fact when religions do come under pressure, particularly of persecution (which has happened to virtually all religions in this century), then religions often find that they can travel extremely light, and can still continue and endure.[34] What we need is a much clearer understanding of where the middle point is (between wanting everything and needing nothing) which will enable strong systems to coexist – an understanding, yet again, of what really are the necessary and indispensable conditions of continuity in each religious case – each, because each will be different: religions with strongly defined constraints over behaviour, such as Judaism or Islam, are likely to be a great deal more specific. But even within such a tradition there will be different evaluations of how much or how little must be maintained and observed. In the terror of Europe there were two main different responses within Judaism to the issue of keeping the commandments of Torah during the holocaust: if the Nazi attack was understood to be an attack on the Jewish religion, then *kiddush haShem*, the sanctification of God's name (a synonym for martyrdom) prevailed; and that is in line with the Talmudic precept (B.San. 74a), that 'one must incur martyrdom, rather than transgress even a minor precept'; but if the attack was on Jews as individuals and communities, then one might invoke *kiddush haHayyim*, the sanctification of life – a phrase attributed to Rabbi Isaac Nissenbaum who nevertheless was killed in the Warsaw ghetto in 1942. On that view it is a duty to save one's own life, and as many other lives as possible; and the *halakoth*, or precepts, of Torah can be interpreted as generously as necessity demands.

So this attempt to specify more clearly and precisely what really *are* the necessary survival conditions as the participants perceive them is by no means simple, because there will not

28

be agreement among the participants. But for that reason it is all the more important to undertake this exercise, otherwise we will never know how they can relate to a secular or neutral environment, let alone to each other. And in any of those particular disputes with which this chapter begins, there cannot be any enduring solution unless the participants 'negotiate down' to that middle point from the high specification of necessity with which they at present live; and such negotiated perception has then to be incorporated in the political and economic and geographical considerations which are equally at issue.

All that, however briefly expressed, has immensely high priority, given the desperate urgency of some of the issues before us. But there are other obvious things to be done as well: one is to recognise the legitimacy of the conflict from the point of view of the participants involved (and that is *not* possible without a knowledge of the points of view of those involved, which itself is not possible without a knowledge of religions). Another is to avoid the language of conflict management and conflict reduction (as though we, paternalistically, from the outside, know how these naughty children ought to behave), while never ignoring the insights which those disciplines and reflections have thrown up. So, for example, there may be pragmatic wisdom in establishing neutral languages and conceptual models through which particular conflicts may be analysed dispassionately. But equally it is essential to remain realistic: in any long-running conflict, there will be those who have a strong interest in its continuing – from superpowers and arms manufacturers down to pathological individuals and individuals seeking revenge.

But on the assumption, as Mo Tzu used to put it, that the majority do wish to live at peace, then certainly it is important to support and reinforce those movements and individuals within which (or whom) is being articulated the internal logic of a particular system which is moving towards resolution, or towards the condemnation of inappropriate (according to its own criteria) violence or aggression. It is not ineffectual idealism to encourage such movements as the World Conference for Religion and Peace (though if that organisation is largely unknown, unavailing and underfunded, it makes the point, once again, about ignorance concerning religions with which this chapter began).

Equally it is important that more people should be, more deliberately, 'multiply religious' (that is, should attempt the marriage, as Bede Griffiths put it, between East and West).[35] That already happens by the accident of paperback publication; at a more serious and deliberately constructive level the attempt to live from different resources is in itself a way of demonstrating the value of coexistence. And perhaps as important as any of the rest, we need to cultivate an *inter*-religious sense of humour. In each religion its believers are capable of humour about themselves and their religion. In any decent-sized bookshop you will find somewhere a book of Jewish humour – not so many books, admittedly, of Muslim humour, or Sikh satire. But *all* these religions generate their own self-deprecating laughter – and in Zen Buddhism such laughter may be a 'royal road' to religious wisdom and insight. But put the religions together, and get a Muslim to tell a joke which deprecates (that is, appears to deprecate) a Jew, or get a Hindu to tell a joke which deprecates a Sikh, and the result will be to reproduce in miniature those larger conflicts which bid fair to destroy us all.

To be able to laugh with each other at ourselves would be an immense gain – but very painful: it was hard enough in adolescence. And a deep problem in inter-religious engagement or dialogue is that religions are immensely unequal in their ability to accept judgment or criticism – let alone initiate it in their own case: the film *The Life of Brian* was an irreverent parody of the life of Jesus, which caused upset for many but which was ultimately healthy for many others, for the quite different way in which it made them see and understand their own appropriation of Christian faith and hope. Imagine what would happen if anything like it were attempted of the life of Muhammad. There was extreme protest in London when an attempt was made to show a highly reverential film of his life. In 1981 an Indian film company was taken to court in Delhi because it showed a scene in a film, *Aanchal*, which showed a Hindu god smoking a cigarette, another god wearing glasses and a third one stammering. A lower court ordered the film to be cut – though the high court in Delhi reinstated the film and allowed the scenes to remain in it.[36]

Of course people are sensitive about sacred things. The whole point of this chapter is to emphasise that religions matter, for many of those who believe, more than anything else; and that is precisely why we have to take them seriously. But religions, often under pressure, have become too over-defensive, too over-sensitive for their own health and happiness, and for their own security. It is for that reason that we need to develop the inter-religious sense of humour, that sense of humour which is so characteristic of the Jews and which has done so much to enable them to survive in more difficult circumstances than most. It is time, for the sake of the peace of so many of the troubled parts of this world, that we all grow up a bit, that we all grow up enough to allow the voice of judgment and criticism and encouragement to be heard, without becoming so defensive that the voice of correction (which all religions need sometimes to hear) is immediately suppressed.

But all or any of these actions require one thing: they require a far better knowledge of religions than most of us – and certainly most of those who make decisions – possess. This chapter has attempted to indicate the pragmatic reasons why we need, not to reduce but to extend and reinforce our self-education about religions. Of the many other reasons, which arise from the way in which religions are the resourceful context of so much good in human life, I have said nothing; but they would certainly reinforce the case. Yet education about religions is exceptionally vulnerable: in the UK it has been a particular victim of the government cuts; and if the UK is of rather minor importance (and requires such education mainly because of the problems and the opportunities of a religiously plural society), then at least one would hope for a more determined attempt to acquire wisdom in the educational systems of the two major powers. But in the USSR and its satellite empire religion is defined in relation to the revolution in such a way that it cannot be taken seriously; and in the USA the separation of Church and State means that only in certain very restricted ways can the role and function of religion be considered. Education is no panacea. As the saying has it, when you have educated the devil, what you have at the end is a clever devil. But education contributes to understanding and wisdom; and if I have appendicitis I would rather be treated by someone who has been medically educated than by one who proceeds by intuition and bedside reading: it is no guarantee of a cure; but it is a contribution to its possibility.

But in addition to these issues of pragmatic urgency and value there are of course issues of truth. It is here that theology arises within the domain of religious studies. The strength of religious systems is derived, not only from (say) their adaptive value as protective cultural packages for gene replication *but also* because they identify (or believe they identify) what they maintain to be true: to be true not only about human nature but also about what they take to be God. But, 'Is there anybody there?' It is one thing to justify the study of religions because of their involvement in so much of what is going on around us. Surely it is quite another thing to defend the worth of reflecting on God as though God is a real being, when we know (do we not?) that there is no such being to be talked about realistically – that is, as though he or she 'really' exists? And would it not be better to accept that our talk about God is in fact concealed talk about (or to) ourselves – our hopes, our fears, our needs, our visionary dreams) So certainly, some have argued; and it is to that issue that we will turn next.

Is There Anybody There?

Religion, according to *The Devil's Dictionary* of Ambrose Bierce, is 'a daughter of Hope and Fear, explaining to Ignorance the nature of the Unknowable'. We have been considering, not religion but religions, in a similar style as licensed insanities; and we have looked at the way in which religions become dangerous precisely because they are so important – particularly because they have been so well-winnowed through time as highly effective cultural programmes for protecting gene replication and the nurture of children, and also because they have initiated and sustained most of the enduring human achievements and discoveries. Of course it is more fashionable to regard religions as infantile insanities (usually without pausing to wonder, for too long, why they have remained so adaptive and persistent through the winnowing process of time). The view of Aldous Huxley (p. 3f) is by no means uncommon; and certainly the general point remains true, that to tell the story of religion is to tell a story that:

> Would harrow up thy soul, freeze thy young blood,
> Make thy two eyes, like stars, start from their spheres,
> Thy knotted and combined locks to part,
> And each particular hair to stand on end,
> Like quills upon the fretful porpentine.[1]

I have not made any attempt to disguise or minimise the unacceptable face of religion. Indeed part of the argument of Chapter 1 was to suggest that in educational terms it is essential to religious education that there should be no evasive apology for religions which circumvents their capacity for violence, terror and destruction. It is precisely because we need to understand *why* that is so, that religious studies should be far more securely integrated into higher education than they are, both in this country and elsewhere.

A small step in the direction of understanding comes when we appreciate why boundary conditions are necessary in any system which is processing information; and why also violent and defensive behaviours are predictable when the information being processed and protected in the system is identified or perceived by participants as non-negotiable – as being, at the furthest limit, more important than the continuation of life itself. Where religions in the UK are concerned this is an issue which has already been faced by many who have come here literally as refugees – fugitives from persecution. When making *Worlds of Faith*, the oldest refugee had fled (with his family) from anti-semitic persecution in Poland in 1911, the youngest were refugees from Tibet and Vietnam. They know at first hand what is at issue in maintaining their faith and life-way; and Mrs Qureshi, a Muslim living in Coventry, spoke for many of them when she said: 'I will never give up my faith . . . Whatever happens, if the worst comes to the worst, my faith cannot be snatched from me. That's a part of my body, that's something attached to my heart, that only dies when I die.'[2]

Although, then, it is clearly false to suggest that religions create nothing but violent and boundary-minded behaviours (since they create also some of the most memorable and moving of human achievements, and they continue to do so as much now in the present as in the past), nevertheless it was the observation of those other impassioned behaviours, so threatening to the world in which we live, which evoked the phrase 'licensed insanities' as a description of religions. That accusation (or as some might prefer, that calm description) is then powerfully reinforced by the fact that religious people not only act, they also speak. It is true that religious people may spend a great deal of their time in silence; but they do also speak sentences; and it is here that the accusations of insanity have been multiplied against them, because so often they seem to be talking realistically about unrealisable, invisible or theoretical entities.

The Anti-Realist Case against God

Examples are not difficult to find: religions talk about god or gods or goddesses; they talk about devils, angels, *jinn*, *asura-s*, *deva-s*. But 'no man hath seen God at any time'.[3] Religions claim also that individuals are constituted not only by flesh and blood and mental behaviours, but also by such realities as soul, *psuche*, *anima*, *neshamah*, *ruh*, *atman*. But no man hath seen the soul at any time. Or to be more accurate, few people. William Blake, in contrast, claimed to have done so: when his brother died, Blake describes how he saw his soul disappear through the ceiling clapping his hands for joy. But that is not a common experience. Then again, religions claim to bring individuals to what are known conventionally as altered or higher states of consciousness, which are clearly not open to direct observation: particular religions will have on offer the *iddhi* power of passing through a mountain, or of levitating round a room, or the shaman's ability to leave his body and visit the domains of the dead; they may even offer slightly more accessible attainments such as *satori*, *samadhi*, *fana*, ecstasy, *wu*, *kavanah*, and the like. Religions also claim to have privileged, and in some cases incorrigible, access to the past through revelation, and to the future through apocalyptic.

All these, in their different ways, are examples of the invisibility of much of the religious subject matter. Religions are certainly not unique in having invisible subject matters – or to put it a bit more precisely, there are theoretical and unseen entities in other domains of human enquiry. Neutrinos in physics would be an example. No man hath seen a neutrino at any time, nor indeed is he likely to do so. Something with no mass, no electric charge, half a unit of spin and travelling at the speed of light is not going to present itself for direct observation very often. Indeed so weakly do neutrinos interact with matter that they pass straight through the earth without a pause for thought, as they could through blocks of lead several light years thick; and in the case of the earth it is highly probable that they will emerge at the exact antipodean point, because the chances of their interacting on the way are less than one in a million million.

So might we perhaps construe those *deva-s* (p. 144) who crowded on the point of a hair around the death-bed of the Buddha, as comparable theoretical entities which do not present themselves to immediate observation? No: they are not comparable, because the intellectual pressure which leads to an inference in physics arises quite differently. The neutrino was first suggested by Pauli to account for an oddity in an entirely different network of discourse and constraint – for the fact that energy was not conserved among the observable particles – and Pauli suggested that this was due to the emission of an invisible 'something', along with the electron, the two sharing the available energy at random. This hypothetical second particle had to be very light and without electric charge, and Pauli originally called it a 'neutron'. When that name was given to the heavier particle discovered by Chadwick in 1932, Pauli's Italian colleagues renamed his hypothetical particle the little neutron, or neutrino. But 'it' was still an inference to account for a problem without sacrificing the principle of the conservation of energy. The hunt was then on for a way of detecting neutrinos, which lasted for a quarter of a century, until Cowan and Reines devised an experiment in 1956 in which the consequences of a neutrino-proton collision could be discerned. Alternatively one could try to detect the flux of solar neutrinos by burying an appropriate tank deep within a gold mine of South Dakota.

What sort of tank do you build to detect the track of a passing angel? Clearly, none at all, because angels are not theoretical entities of that sort. But then perhaps they are not entities of any sort; and perhaps theological language (language about God) is really a different kind of language, not meant to be quasi-realistic, but rather addressed to ourselves for the purposes of exhortation or of encouraging our altruistic insight:

> Which of us has seen a spirit?
> We have no belief to bring us near it:
> Yet in the world of poetry
> We can admit such things may be,
> And in the possibility
> Receive enlarged experience
> Of beauty and the interior sense
> Of man's most intimate dealing with man.[5]

Perhaps indeed we should regard theology as a kind of poetry, not intended (if we are wise) to describe an object, or putative object, as realistically as possible but rather to evoke and nurture our imagination of ourselves, our cosmos and our responsibilities.

The idea that religious language might be better understood as poetic was flirted with by an Anglican doctrine commission in its report, *Christian Believing*. It was not espoused in the main body of the report (p. 19), but the chairman of the commission kept its hopes alive in his own personal contribution: 'Language about God, as we have emphasised in our report, is necessarily indirect – even poetic in character, a word with which I am much less unhappy than the report as a whole' (p. 126).

But the issue of realism will still return in the form of a question, 'indirect about what?' Certainly much poetry is religious and theological, and much religion and theology is expressed in poetic language. But what, still, is it language about? 'Poetic truth' does not stand on its own, as a kind of artistic Crusoe on an island bereft of all reference and communciation – as the analysis of Robin Skelton makes clear, in a book to which he gave that very title, poetic truth. He argued that, 'the structure of poetry is, in all respects, an exact presentation of the nature of human perception, and that it conveys to the sensitive reader a remarkably precise picture of the situation of man with regard to his apprehensions of time, history, evolution, language, and the world "outside" him.'[6]

But those are all thoroughly realistic concerns. 'Exact presentations', 'remarkably precise pictures' and 'the world "outside" ' are phrases which belong naturally (naturalistically) to the immense discussions throughout virtually all centuries to which we have access, about whether our languages describe (or attempt to describe) what exists to be described (whether we happen to be here to make the attempt or not), or whether our languages are expressions of our own understanding which construct the worlds in which we live in the ways that make them livable.

The issue, in that respect, is thus very much as Cupitt proposed, when he was *Taking Leave of God:*

The realists stick to what they say is commonsense and

tradition. They say that the existence of God is in the end a factual question. One who believes in God must maintain that there exists a certain distinct and independent Spirit, the creator and ruler of all things, unsurpassable in power, wisdom and goodness, who would exist and be exactly the same even if nobody believed in him any longer and even if there was no world at all . . .

The other group, the expressionists, hold that the God of realism does not in fact exist but is an illusion created by a misunderstanding of the nature of religious language. They hold that religious language is basically expressive in force, not descriptive. God's reality is not a matter of facts and evidence, but of the unconditional authority of religious categories in a person's life.[7]

Why such categories should have authority is an obvious question. As it stands, Cupitt's position might reinforce the case for religious studies in an educational system, but certainly not for theology. If theology is not 'about' anything except the refinement and aesthetics of human sensibility, it might be better accommodated in the equivalent of a finishing school for those who can afford not to live in a real world. It would have some place in the archaeology of knowledge, as one ponders the intellectual universe in which 'our ancestors invented an emblematic botany, a natural history composed of allegories and fables, an astronomy that told fortunes and illustrated the dogmas of revealed religion'.[8] Theology would still be shaking, as Dotty puts it to Tom Stoppard's George Moore, 'from the 400 year old news that the sun doesn't go round *you!*' Moore comments: 'We are *all* still shaking. Copernicus cracked our confidence, and Einstein smashed it: for if one can no longer believe that a twelve-inch ruler is always a foot long, how can one be sure of relatively less certain propositions, such as that God made the Heaven and the Earth?'[9]

There is in that statement excessive dramatic licence. But such, in miniature, is Cupitt's position, particularly in the television series and subsequent book, *The Sea of Faith:*

The shift, then, is from myths to maths, from animism to mechanism, and from explanation down from above to explanation up from below . . . Realism is long dead and gone: we live in a time when religion has become fully human, when theology is like art, and when we use the available resources as aids to our own spiritual formation, but must in the last resort find each of us his own unique voice.[10]

The fundamental point of the antirealist in the case of theology is that there is no objective being in a higher world, as Cupitt puts it, correctly referred to as God. There is no such objective being. Consequently there cannot (obviously) be any descriptive, realistic languages about God because there is nothing there or anywhere so to be described.

So theology as a would-be descriptive language is out, a plain impossibility. Therefore we have to ask what all the ferment of theological language is *really* about. The answer given is that it is about ourselves. It is addressed to ourselves as what Cupitt calls 'present imperatives'. Theological language is a concealed present imperative, a powerful exhortation to ourselves to behave more spiritually, more responsibly, more accountably, more lovingly, and so on: 'In recent centuries the factual or descriptive elements of belief have been steadily whittled away until nothing serious is left of them. When the purge is complete we see that spirituality is everything. Doctrines that used to be regarded as describing supernatural facts are now seen as prescribing a supernatural mode of existence.'[11]

In that case, as he concludes, 'all religious doctrines and themes become present imperatives, which if they are functioning properly and with their full force simply cure the believer of anxiety'. Now clearly a nurse or doctor may also offer a hot sweet cup of tea to someone to alleviate the immediate crisis of anxiety. But if a doctor or psychiatrist attempts, over a longer term, to cure someone of anxiety she or he usually pays considerable attention to the facts (so far as they can be discerned) which underlie the patient's language about symptoms and anxieties. Theological language has traditionally done exactly the same. The language has been of effect, not only because it can occasionally be written in fine poetry (not least, on occasion, in hymns) but also because it appeals to what it takes to be the case. So it is an obvious problem in Cupitt's account that the majority of theological sentences do not look in the least like present imperatives, nor, for that matter, like poetry. Exactly the opposite: they look like sentences about supposed (or to use the jargon, putative) matters of fact.

This was a point made very strongly by Clement Webb, when he was raising doubts about William James' version of pragmatism. Having emphasised the great service, as he put it, which 'is done to the philosophy of religion when it is pointed out that a religious proposition cannot be treated as taking its place side by side with the propositions which are found in a treatise of natural science or history', he went on:

> But this association of pragmatism with a fruitful line of theological thought is not sufficient to enable it to give a satisfactory form to religious conviction. The question why religious dogma naturally assumes a form of expression more like that appropriate to a scientific assertion than that which we use in our moral and aesthetic judgements still demands an answer. The strength of scholasticism . . . always lay and still lies in its stress upon the independent nature of the object of knowledge.[12]

The same point has been made more recently, and with equal vigour, by Donald Mackay, whose own work lies within the natural sciences, rather than in the history of ideas:

> The burden of the Christian religion is not primarily that certain attitudes are desirable nor that certain practices are comfortable, but that certain things are true. Certain facts have to be faced, certain claims recognised . . . However much emphasis we give to the vital link between true belief and action – and for the Bible the two are inseparable – there is no escaping the obligation to enquire into the meaning and truth of Christian affirmations, as well as their personal or social effectiveness.[13]

Manifestly Cupitt does not provide the answer that Webb was looking for. He simply asserts, without argument, that there is no independent nature of the object of knowledge in the case of God. Consequently 'God' is an entirely human construction, in which the needs of our spiritual nature have been projected outside ourselves and falsely reified (made into a 'thing', an object), although there is no such object in reality. So he states: 'People once thought of God as an objective being in a higher world, but now we realise that the only true God is *our* God, the religious idea.' Consequently, 'the admission is now inescapable that religion is entirely human, made by men for men'[14] – exactly indeed as the feminists always suspected, though no doubt Cupitt meant something rather different by the phrase.

What he certainly did mean was that all ways of human thinking about anything are human constructions; and at this point he is espousing the very prevalent and widespread view that the worlds we approach in thought or language are not 'really there': they become what we make them through the instrument and convention of the language, the concepts and the pictures which we use. Hence have arisen what are known as instrumentalism and conventionalism in the history and philosophy of science and in the sociology of knowledge, in which knowledge is always relative to particular persons and places, cultural contexts and moments in history. Claims to knowledge cannot be evaluated from some independent, Archimedean point of realism (by asking to what extent they *correspond* to what is really the case, as though what is really the case can be independently known from some other, neutral, point of view), because we do not know what is really (realistically) the case outside *our own* contextualised and relative ways of deciding the matter. That is why Barnes and Bloor arrived at their 'equivalence postulate', which claims:

> that all beliefs are on a par with one another with respect to the causes of their credibility; it is not that all beliefs are equally true or equally false, but that regardless of truth and falsity the fact of their credibility is to be seen as equally problematic; the position we shall defend is that the incidence of all beliefs without exception calls for empirical investigation and must be accounted for by finding the specific, local causes of this credibility.[15]

They then pressed home the point in this way:

> For the relativist there is no sense attached to the idea that some standards or beliefs are really rational as distinct from merely locally accepted as such. Because he thinks that there are no context-free or super-cultural norms of

41

rationality, he does not see rationally and irrationally held beliefs as making up two distinct and qualitatively different classes of thing. They do not fall into two different natural kinds which make different sorts of appeal to the human mind, or stand in a different relationship to reality, or depend for their credibility on different patterns of social organisation. Hence the relativist conclusion that they are to be explained in the same way.[16]

From that, it follows, according to Kuhn and Feyerabend (see further on p. 51f) that competing theories in science are necessarily incommensurable, since there is nothing outside themselves against which to judge them. If we then add to that consideration the attack launched by Sellars on the 'myth of the given', Quine's assault on the two dogmas of empiricism, and the realisation that theories are in any case radically underdetermined, it will be clear how far some philosophers (and especially some philosophers of science) have moved away from a view that science proceeds simply (or fairly simply) in the direction of knowing and describing what is really there in the universe, waiting for us to stumble across it.[17]

An implication of instrumental understandings of knowledge is that whatever the universe may ultimately be like in itself, we can only know it through our theories, language, models and equations. None of these is able to reproduce the whole of what there really is, out there, waiting, as it were, to be described. We can only construct through our pictures or theories (whether of common sense or of science) how it seems to us. Half a century ago the physicist and cosmologist Arthur Eddington began his Gifford lectures on *The Nature of the Physical World* by asking: Is this table a comparatively permanent, coloured and substantial object, or is it a swarm of atoms which is nearly all empty space? It is of course both – and more than both – depending on the human context in which we encounter what we call a table, and our purposes in using or examining it. If we are sitting at it to write a letter or eat a meal, or appreciating the style of Chippendale furniture, our descriptions of the table will be quite different – but no less valid – than those we would construct in a laboratory while studying the micro-structure of mahogany or the behaviour of carbon isotopes. As the physicist Henry Margenau once put the extreme position aggressively, 'The physicist does not discover, he creates his universe.'

It is clear that Cupitt intended to adopt this general point of view – though it is not so clear that he has followed through the very sharp refinements which have been compelled upon it by the debates of the last two decades, since he does give to the natural sciences (without much consideration of the point) a paradigm perspective, which is precisely what the instrumentalists and conventionalists have called in question. Nevertheless, he argues:

> As the body of available scientific knowledge and technology grows ever larger and more powerful, science progressively takes over from religion, in one area of life after another, the task of explaining what is happening and prescribing what is to be done. Even in fields whose precise scientific status is disputed, such as economics, social science and psychology, it is still the case that secular, utilitarian and 'engineering' or instrumental ways of thinking have taken over.[18]

Where theology is concerned, this is clearly the crux of the matter. If instrumentalism (if, that is, the view that our languages and theories are instruments through which we construct our different worlds, which have no necessary or determinative contact with an accessible reality apart from those languages), if instrumentalism has banished realism even from the sciences, must it not do so even more, or at least just as much, in theology? If science has abandoned all hope of describing realistically what is lying out there waiting passively for us to describe it, then clearly theology has no hope of describing realistically even less visible 'entities' like God (supposing, for the moment, that God can be regarded in that way). But has science actually done that? Has science abandoned realism and gone over to instrumentalism in the thorough-going way that Cupitt supposes? And even if it has, does it have the implications that he suggests? Only if that is so can the shift from realism in the natural sciences be applied destructively to the elimination of realistic language in theology.

What is certainly true – and this clearly gives strong

preliminary support to Cupitt's view – is that there *has* been in the last 100 years a complete revolution – a dramatic reversal from the widespread ambition in the nineteenth century to achieve complete and realistic descriptions of what lies out there waiting to be described – a revolution from that kind of realistic ambition to an acceptance that such complete, correspondent accounts cannot ever be achieved, and that subjective interpretation is both paramount and is limited by the language or technique of the context in which it occurs: our languages are indeed instruments with which we construct the worlds in which we live. It is an immense revolution. It is not altogether easy for us to discern it, because we happen to be living right in the middle of it – or rather, as now appears to be the case, at the very end of it. Nevertheless it has been a profound revolution, and one which has occurred not just in the natural sciences but in virtually every manifestation of human reflection, enquiry and creativity, whether in art, music, sculpture, ethics, fiction, drama, history – though not (and this is important) in such enterprises as cooking or engineering.

To the extent that there has been this revolution from realism to subjectivism or expressionism, in so many different fields, Cupitt is superficially on the side of the angels (or would be, supposing, from the anti-realist point of view, that there are any). So important has this revolution been that it is worth spending a moment looking at some examples of what it has meant. But then I want to suggest that the revolution has not been so absolute in its consequences as Cupitt appears to suppose; and in so far as the realism/anti-realism debate is still very much alive, it is clearly premature to declare in relation to theology that 'realism is dead'.

From Realism to Subjectivism: the Eclipse of an Ambition in the Sciences

In 1960 Charles Gillispie published a book called *The Edge of Objectivity*, in which he reviewed the consequences – the growing edge – of the ambition to create an objective description of nature, based on the success of the Newtonian mechanistic revolution. It offered the hope that all phenomena could be embraced under laws as specifiable and universal as gravity – not only the universe but also *l'homme machine*.[19] The task of slaying the chimera of superstition and religion was as exhilarating a century ago as it is now to the anti-realism of Cupitt:

> The true world which science reveals to us is much superior to the fantastic world created by the imagination . . . In vain we have inflated our conceptions, we have only fathered fragments at the enormous price of the reality of things. Is it not a strange fact that all the ideas by which primitive science explained the world appear to us narrow, paltry, ridiculous next to those which are true? . . . Therefore let us say without fear that if fiction's marvels seemed up to now necessary for poetry, nature's marvels when laid bare in all their splendour will constitute a poetry a thousand times more sublime, a poetry which will be reality itself, which will be science and philosophy simultaneously.[20]

So Ernest Renan, in the middle of the nineteenth century. But the Newtonian ambition was not confined to him alone. Michelson (of the Michelson-Morley experiment)[21] remarked in 1894 that the future of science would consist of 'adding a few decimal places to results already obtained'[22] – though admittedly he later withdrew that remark.

Others were not so modest; and in their view, such a comprehensive and realistic account would leave no room for theology at all – just as Cupitt leaves no room for theology of any serious kind, but *he* does so on the basis of instrumentalism! John Tyndall (the very anti-theistic physicist whom Mallock put into *The New Republic*) made exactly this claim in his address to the British Association in Belfast in 1874: 'The impregnable position of science may be described in a few words. We claim, and we shall wrest from theology, the entire domain of cosmological theory. All schemes and systems which thus infringe upon the domain of science must, insofar as they do this, submit to its control, and relinquish all thought of controlling it.'[23]

But since those heady days of realism what is inescapably obvious is that we have to take account of what we may appropriately call (in counterpoint to Gillispie) the edge of subjectivity – the recognition, in so many different fields of enquiry and reflection, that the realistic ambition cannot be achieved. To see the point let us suppose that, by some trick of time, we could take our seats in the lecture theatre of the Royal Institution of London on a Friday afternoon in April in the year 1900. Supposing we could have done that, we would then have been able to hear Lord Kelvin deliver his celebrated lecture, 'Nineteenth Century Clouds over the Dynamical Theory of Heat and Light'. Why so celebrated? Because Lord Kelvin was drawing attention to the last two remaining clouds, or impediments, which were blocking the way to the completion of a thorough-going Newtonian account of what the universe is and how it works – a realistic description of what lies out there, waiting to be described; a universe which, because of the universality of its specifiable and invariant laws, would have to be regarded as determined and deterministic. T. H. Huxley wrote of the same John Tyndall: 'A favourite problem of his is – Given the molecular forces in a mutton chop, deduce Hamlet or Faust therefrom. He is confident that the Physics of the Future will solve this easily.'[24]

That was simply a flamboyant expression of the widespread realistic ambition which so many scientists shared. What Kelvin perceived was that there were two intransigent puzzles which were standing in the way of completing that realistic description of what the universe is and how it works in Newtonian terms. So near and yet so far, because the two questions which Kelvin refused to evade were first, how can the earth move through 'an elastic solid such as essentially is the luminiferous ether';[25] and second, how is it possible to account for 'the Maxwell-Boltzmann doctrine regarding the partition of energy'.

Both of those may seem remote as problems. But the first drew attention to the Michelson-Morley experiment, which had shown that the speed of light is not affected by the direction in which the source-object of the light happens to be travelling. If the ether exists (the ether having been postulated to exist in order that the light waves of Newtonian theory could have something through which to propagate), then in Newtonian terms there should be some effect of the ether on the speed of light. Fitzgerald and then Lorentz had tried to rescue the ether by supposing a foreshortening of the apparatus of the Michelson-Morley experiment in the direction of its own motion, which would thus equalise the direct and the transverse movements. But Kelvin, although he referred to it as 'a brilliant suggestion',[26] was aware that it was a desperate expedient. He observed: 'I cannot see any flaw either in the idea or in the execution . . . of this experiment . . . I am afraid we must still regard Cloud No. 1 as very dense.'[27]

Cloud No. 2 arose from the success of Maxwell (see p. 76) and Boltzmann in using statistical mechanics to produce results of persuasive simplicity and generality in relation particularly to the behaviour of molecules of gas, subject to the mechanical laws of collision. The detail of the consequent problem cannot really be summarised in a sentence. But the consequences in relation to the Newtonian ambition *have* been summarised by Otto Frisch in this way:

> Apparently atoms behave as if they were rigidly connected with their neighbours when the temperature is low, but as it gets warmer and the energy of thermal agitation goes up, an increasing proportion of that energy is absorbed by the oscillation of the atoms until the amount demanded by the equipartition theorem is accounted for. Such behaviour on the part of the atoms may be thoroughly sensible, but it contradicts the laws of classical physics. The equipartition theorem . . . follows mathematically from the general laws of Newtonian mechanics. Its consequences do not agree with the experiments, so the laws of Newtonian mechanics are not correct and must be replaced by something else.[28]

It was because the experimental data were at odds with the theoretical laws of Newtonian mechanics that Lord Rayleigh (an unwavering adherent to the work of Maxwell and Boltzmann) was reduced to saying – and Kelvin quoted him at the end of his lecture: 'What would appear to be wanted is some escape from the destructive simplicity of the general conclusion'; on which Kelvin commented: 'The simplest way of arriving at this desired result is to deny the conclusion; and so, in the beginning of the twentieth century, to lose sight of a cloud which has obscured the brilliance of the molecular theory of heat and light during the last quarter of the nineteenth century.'[29]

But there was no denying the conclusion; and Rayleigh's word 'destructive' was entirely right; for these two clouds were the two classic points at which the ambition to complete a realistic Newtonian account of the universe was shown to be impossible. The first cloud, because of its dependence on the Michelson-Morley experiment, was signalling Einsteinian relativity; and the second, by opening up the possibility that statistical behaviour may be inherent in the elementary processes of the universe itself, pointed to the uncertainty principle which was to become so decisive in the forming of quantum mechanics.

It is true that the quantum world was actually more directly signalled by another lecture in 1900, the equally celebrated one, given by Max Planck to the German Physical Society, in which he solved what is known as the ultraviolet catastrophe, by proposing that matter absorbs heat energy and emits light-energy discretely – in discrete packets which came to be known, from the Latin, as *quanta* – hence quantum mechanics.[30] But Kelvin was right – and his lecture stands as one of the great monuments to human integrity, since although he could not propose solutions he refused to countenance the adjustments and manipulations of others who were attempting to accommodate the data to the prevailing theories and ambitions. Like stout Cortez (and he was by then of more robust build than he had been), he saw a new planet – or rather, a new universe – swimming into his ken. He was on the threshold of the universe in which we now live, in which we have to accept the relativity of our observations, and also the fact that at the quantum level it is impossible, not just in theory but in principle, to give a complete and realistic description of both the position and the velocity or related properties of an electron or similar small body. From a view which regarded the entire universe, in all its detail, as a vast machine, of such regularity that if the state and position of all its components at any one moment could be known it would be possible to predict its whole future unfolding, it is now clear that that is impossible, not just in practice, but in principle. At the quantum level (describing and explaining physical phenomena below the dimensions of atoms), a complete description of the universe and of the behaviour of all its parts becomes in principle impossible.[31] We 'disturb the universe' when we observe it at this level: in making one measurement (of momentum) it becomes impossible to make the other related observation (of position) or vice versa; or to invert the point, the state of a particle has a meaning only when a precise procedure for observing the state is prescribed.

On this, the physicist Freeman Dyson commented (in a book whose title, *Disturbing the Universe*, underlines the point):

> Among physicists there are many different philosophical viewpoints, and many different ways of interpreting the role of the observer in the description of sub-atomic processes. But all physicists agree with the experimental facts which make it hopeless to look for a description independent of the mode of observation. When we are dealing with things as small as atoms and electrons, the observer or experimenter cannot be excluded from the description of nature.[32]

It is in this sense, and at this level, that the term 'participant universe' has been coined, to emphasise the distinction between what is now the case (as Freeman Dyson has described it) and the old realistic ambition of the nineteenth century, of describing what is going on 'out there', whether we are here to observe it or not: the observer is now, at the quantum level, within the observation. Others, of course, have put the matter more extremely: John Gribbin has produced a book, *In Search of Schrödinger's Cat* in which according to the sub-title, 'the startling world of quantum physics is explained'. In this, there is a claim which is indeed very startling: 'What quantum mechanics says is that nothing is real.'[33] That is to do for physics what Cupitt had done for theology; and, I shall want to argue, with no justification in either case.

Nevertheless the shift to Einsteinian relativity and to quantum mechanics illustrates the growing edge of subjectivity. For if we have indeed moved from an observer-observed universe to a participant universe, then perhaps we participate in the construction of *all* our universes: maybe, all our worlds are conventional constructions, as Poincaré was already affirming of geometry. That was also startling: for what could be more realistic than Euclidean geometry mapping an external space in terms of its relationships? But the development of alternative, non-Euclidean geometries seemed to suggest that all such formal systems are human constructions which have to be evaluated by their own axioms and rules, and that in themselves they say nothing at all about the structure of physical space. Thus in a particularly famous paper, 'The Unreasonable Effectiveness of Mathematics in the Natural Sciences', the physicist Eugene Wigner was able to defend the position that basic theoretical constructions may rest on incompatible mathematical concepts:

> We now have, in physics, two theories of great power and interest: the theory of quantum phenomena and the theory of relativity. These two theories have their roots in mutually exclusive groups of phenomena. Relativity theory applies to macroscopic bodies, such as stars. The event of coincidence, that is, in ultimate analysis, of collision, is the primitive event in the theory of relativity and defines a point in space-time, or at least would define a point if the colliding particles were infinitely small. Quantum theory has its roots in the microscopic world and, from its point of view, the event of coincidence, or of collision, even if it takes place between particles of no spatial extent, is not primitive and not at all sharply isolated in space-time. The two theories operate with different mathematical concepts – the four dimensional Riemann space and the infinite dimensional Hilbert space, respectively. So far, the two theories could not be united, that is, no mathematical formulation exists to which both of these theories are approximations. All physicists believe that a union of the two theories is inherently possible and that we shall find it. Nevertheless, it is possible also to imagine that no union of the two theories can be found.

The conclusion that some draw from this, in an anti-realist direction, is not that geometry and mathematics are arbitrary, but that they proceed by the establishment of human consensus, not by the demonstration of their correspondence to some independent reality. This is exactly the argument of an influential book by Davis and Hersh (and some others) on *The Mathematical Experience:* 'Mathematics is not the study of an ideal, pre-existing non-temporal reality. Neither is it a chess-like game with made-up symbols and formulas. Rather, it is the part of human studies which is capable of achieving a science-like consensus.'[34]

From this they draw yet another startling conclusion, that mathematics is one of the world's great religions – and in this, the collapse of the realistic ambition is explicit:

> Mathematics does have a subject matter, and its statements are meaningful. The meaning of mathematics however is to be found in the shared understanding of human beings not in an external non-human reality. In this respect, mathematics is similar to an ideology, a religion or an art form. It deals with human meanings, and is intelligible only within the context of culture. In other words, mathematics is a humanistic study. It is one of the humanities.[35]

If enterprises which appear to be so realistic (geometry and mathematics) can be argued to be human constructions, without *necessary* relation to 'reality', then perhaps *everything* is a human invention – not just God, but even those regularities which seem so inevitably real that they are actually called 'the laws of nature'. That was precisely the conclusion (or more precisely, the point of departure) of Robert Pirsig in a book which, in its day, enjoyed a wide circulation, *Zen and the Art of Motorcycle Maintenance* (p. 34): 'Laws of nature are human inventions like ghosts. Laws of logic, of mathematics are also human inventions, like ghosts. The whole blessed thing is a human invention, including the idea that it *isn't* a human invention. The world has no existence whatsoever outside the human imagination.'

That may sound extreme, but it is, in its own way, a dramatic statement of the revolution in the philosophy of science which Kuhn and Feyerabend focused in 1962. In that year occurred what David Papineau called recently, an overnight sensation: 'If philosophy had overnight sensations,' he claimed, 'this would have been one.'[36] Why? Because it was the year in which a book and an article appeared, in which the anti-realist case was made with extreme vigour. The book was Kuhn's, *The Structure of Scientific Revolutions*. Its main argument was not in itself anti-realist, since it observed, simply, that natural sciences proceed normally by puzzle-solving within scientific communities on the assumption of commonly accepted theories which Kuhn called 'paradigms' – a particularly unfortunate word, the meaning of which Kuhn changed (like Humpty Dumpty) at least three times. When anomalies arise (an example would be Kelvin's Two Clouds) which cannot be solved within the prevailing paradigms, there then occurs a revolutionary break – or 'paradigm shift'.

In itself, this is not anti-realist. It only became so when it was claimed that the preference for one theory over another is determined, *not* by one being a better representation than the other of what nature is really like, but by utilitarian or aesthetic considerations, or simply by approval in particular communities. Kuhn certainly gave the impression of espousing that conclusion, although with question-marks which he has subsequently reinforced, virtually to the extent of returning to a critically realist position. Nevertheless, his first hints were in that opposite, relativist, direction:

> We are all deeply accustomed to seeing science as the one enterprise that draws constantly nearer to some goal set by nature in advance. But need there be such a goal? Can we not account for both science's existence and its success in terms of evolution from the community's state of knowledge at any given time? Does it really help to imagine that there is some one full, objective, true account of nature and that the proper measure of scientific achievement is the extent to which it brings us closer to that ultimate goal?[37]

The hesitations of those question-marks were not shared by Feyerabend. His article of the same year, 'Explanation, Reduction and Empiricism', was a first shot in a long campaign in which he has pressed home exactly the relativist conclusion. His book, *Against Method*, is subtitled 'Towards an Anarchistic Theory of Knowledge', and here, as elsewhere, he takes the view that science is more like a church than a rational enterprise, and that its theories are no closer to 'final truth' than are the myths and fairy-tales of popular culture: 'The epistemological anarchist . . . has no objection to regarding the fabric of the world as described by science and revealed by his senses as a chimera that either conceals a deeper and, perhaps, spiritual reality, or as a mere web of dreams that reveals, and conceals, nothing.'[38]

These are the extreme voices of anti-realism. It is certainly *not* the case (as we shall see) that there are no other voices to be heard – that all physicists, all mathematicians, all philosophers of science proclaim, as Cupitt does for theology, that 'realism is dead'. But the purpose of quoting these examples is to emphasise how dramatic the shift, from the pervasive nineteenth-century ambition to achieve realistic accounts, has been.

From Realism to Subjectivism: the Eclipse of an Ambition in the Arts

What certainly reinforces Cupitt's anti-realism (at least initially) is that that 'revolution' from realism to subjectivism has taken place in many other fields of human creativity and enquiry. The nineteenth-century ambition to achieve realistic accounts is just as easy to find elsewhere: it is precisely what Hawthorne liked most about the novels of Trollope:

> They precisely suit my taste – solid and substantial, written on the strength of beef and through the inspiration of ale, and just as real as if some giant had hewn a great lump out of the earth, and put it under a glass case, with all its inhabitants going about their daily business, and not suspecting that they were being made a show of.

It was that same sort of ambition that led Charles Reade to employ undergraduates to dig archaeologically in the Bodleian Library, so that his novel, *The Cloister and the Hearth*, might the more faithfully reproduce the Middle Ages as they must have been in experience for those who were alive at the time. It is the equivalent of what the Goncourt brothers called (and attempted, both in their novels and their more famous Journal) '*l'autopsie perpetuelle et journalière de son être*' – a constant and daily autopsy of one's being.

As with the sciences and mathematics, so also here, it is *not* the case that every author or every artist in the nineteenth century was a realist: realism and naturalism are identifiable concerns in a period which also produced that non-realism which Roberts-Jones aptly called 'beyond time and place',[39] and symbolism – whose central claim Jean Moréas summarised in the *Symbolist Manifesto* (1886) in this way: 'Symbolic poetry, opposed to "teaching, declamation, false sensibility, objective description", seeks to clothe the idea in a perceptible form.'[40]

But in contrast to that, the many forms of realism which did seek objective description were far more pervasive. George Eliot, in her deliberate case for realism embedded in the middle of *Adam Bede* (in the chapter 'In Which the Story Pauses a Little'!), had summarised the views of many on the divine or perceptible form:

> All honour and reverence to the divine beauty of form! Let us cultivate it to the utmost in men, women, and children – in our gardens and in our houses. But let us love that other beauty too, which lies in no secret of proportion, but in the secret of deep human sympathy. Paint us an angel, if you can, with a floating violet robe, and a face paled by the celestial light; paint us yet oftener a Madonna, turning her mild face upward and opening her arms to welcome the divine glory; but do not impose on us any aesthetic rules which shall banish from the region of Art those old women scraping carrots with their work-worn hands, those heavy clowns taking holiday in a dingy pot-house, those rounded backs and stupid weather-beaten faces that have bent over the spade and done the rough work of the world – those homes with their tin pans, their brown pitchers, their rough curs, and their clusters of onions. In this world there are so many of these common coarse people, who have no picturesque sentimental wretchedness! It is so needful we should remember their existence, else we may happen to leave them quite out of our religion and philosophy, and frame lofty theories which only fit a world of extremes. Therefore let Art always remind us of them; therefore let us always have men ready to give the loving pains of a life to the faithful representing of commonplace things . . .

It was precisely that kind of realism which Courbet proclaimed only three years before the publication of *Adam Bede:* 'Painting is an essentially *concrete* art and can only consist of the presentation of *real and existing things*. It is a completely physical language, the words of which consist of all visible objects.' In an echo of George Eliot, he once replied to a request to paint a religious picture, 'Show me an angel and I will paint one! Painting is an art of sight.'

Courbet therefore confined the realist painter to the *contemporary* scene. In his view it is not possible to paint a scene purporting to have occurred in the past, because the artist was not there to observe it – in other words it is *not* a work of imagination. *'Il faut être de son temps'*, was a succinct way of summarising the point. But others, not least the Pre-Raphaelites, who first met as the Brotherhood in 1848, *were* prepared to be realistic about the past: they were prepared to paint the scene in the past as it would have been if the artist had been a spectator at the time. They expressed, artistically, the equivalent of J. S. Mill's epistemology, in which he avoided discussion of what there needs to be ontologically for justified claims to knowledge to be made, when he spoke of Permanent Possibilities of Sensation: 'I believe that Calcutta exists, though I do not perceive it, and that it would still exist if every percipient inhabitant were suddenly to leave the place, or be struck dead . . . The Permanent Possibility of Sensation which I call Calcutta would still remain.' The equivalent of this epistemological realism led to the Pre-Raphaelites 'putting into paint' something akin to Ranke's later dictum, that the task of a historian is to present the event as it really was at the time.

What that also meant for the Pre-Raphaelites was a ferocious attention to detail, to create the impression that the spectator was looking into an actual scene – not always with happy results, as Linda Nochlin has observed: 'For the Pre-Raphaelites, Realism – *plein-air* or otherwise – implied an earnest, painstaking accuracy, a commitment to hard work shared in common with the aspiring middle-classes of their country, and an insistence on the recording of minute details which tended both to congeal or embalm the subject for posterity . . .'[41]

But the paintings, coherent as they were with the widespread realistic ambitions of the time in other fields, impressed others deeply. On one of the key paintings of the movement, Holman Hunt's 'Strayed Sheep' (a painting which Ruskin regarded as having changed his understanding of art), Ruskin commented: 'For the first time in the history of art [is shown] the absolutely faithful balance of colour and shade by which actual sunshine is transported into a key in which the harmonies possible with material pigments should yet produce the same impressions upon the mind which were caused by the light itself . . .'[42]

But what actually is the reality which realism was attempting to convey? It was in relation to that question that the ground began to tremble beneath their feet, as it was trembling beneath the feet of Lord Kelvin in physics. That phrase of Ruskin's, 'the transportation of actual sunshine', is almost exactly the same as the one used by Zola to describe the artists we now know as the Impressionists. The Impressionists were as bitterly opposed to the Pre-Raphaelites as some of the Pre-Raphaelites were opposed to the Impressionists. Yet Zola could write of the Impressionists in almost exactly the same way: 'Here then is what the Impressionist painters exhibit, exact research into the causes and effects of light flowing in upon the design as well as upon the colour . . . life as it is, rendered in its actual conditions of light.'[43]

The fact that it was Zola who made that comment is important, because Zola regarded himself as an equivalent realist in literature, the scientist who observes life and then conducts experiments on his characters: he is not concerned to draw moral conclusions, but only to exhibit life as it is. To him therefore the Impressionists were to be admired as realists, as the Pre-Raphaelites were to Ruskin; and their judgments on the effect of light sound very similar. Yet in fact the Impressionists had made the all-important move, by recognising that the reality to be recorded is not 'out there', but 'in here', within the perceiving, experiencing artist. There is nothing 'out there' to be 'congealed and passed on to posterity': there is only the transient impression of the passing scene.

From there, it was an obvious conclusion to be drawn that there is not even a simple, fixed impression of a scene or object, but a rapidly fleeting sequence of impressions. Van Gogh was as much prepared as any earlier Impressionist 'to express the values of crowds', as he put it in a letter to Ridder van Rappard, 'and to separate things in the dizzy whirl and chaos one can see in each little corner of Nature'. But he was then equally prepared to rearrange nature in order to capture the multiplicity of its limitless effect:

> When I once *get the feeling of my subject* and get to know it, I usually draw it in three or more variations – be it a figure or a landscape – only I always refer to Nature for every one of them and then I do my best never to put in *any detail*, as the dream quality would then be lost.[44]

The 'dream quality': it is in that way that Impressionism was eroded by Post-Impressionism; for then, why not attempt to capture the multiplicity of any supposed subject, not in a succession of different pictures, but with the whole multiplicity of possible impressions in a single work? And that is how we arrive at the endeavour (often the long endeavour, through many years) of Picasso to portray on a flat surface the three main impressions of a three-dimensional object – as in his series of paintings of a violin.

His first attempts represent still the *addition* of complexity, not the logical simplicity of the underlying constitutive structure. Picasso saw the point himself. He said in a conversation in 1934:

> Formerly pictures used to move towards completion in progressive stages. Each day would bring something new. A picture was a sum of additions. But with me a picture is a sum of destructions. I do a picture, then I destroy it. But in the long run nothing is lost; the red that I took away from one place always turns up somewhere else.[45]

In the four stages of his lithograph of a bull[46] it is possible to see this process at work, as the conception moves towards increasing simplicity of suggestive line. But in that process one can see the kind of interior logic through which this increasing move away from realism developed into Cubism, with its attempt to capture all the angles or impressions of an object, but in the most simplified form which a flat surface makes necessary. Initially in Cubism complexity persists, as one can see in the early Picasso nudes, or in such paintings by Georges Braque as 'A View of Montmartre from his Studio'; of which two productions one might well say '*vive la différence*', supposing one could actually tell it. What they both retain is the three-dimensional illusion of angle and of depth. Why not simplify that even further, to that basic, necessary, structural line, and accept that the flat plane of a canvas surface demands a corresponding plane-like (but dynamic) display of relationship? The result is exemplified in the geometrical shapes and lines of Mondrian in another view of Paris, 'La Place de la Concorde'. From there it is a relatively short stop, even further from realism, to the pile of bricks on the floor of the Tate Gallery[47] and to the question of Nelson Goodman, *not*, as we are usually inclined to put it, '*What* is art?' but the question '*When* is art'[48] To put it in his own words: 'A non-representational picture such as a Mondrian says nothing, denotes nothing, pictures nothing, and is neither true nor false, but shows much.'[49] Or to invert the point:

> A passage or picture may exemplify or express without describing or representing, and even without being a description or representation at all – as in the case of some passages from James Joyce and some drawings by Kandinsky . . . Emphasis on the denotative (representative or descriptive), the exemplificatory ('formal' or 'decorative'), and the expressive in the arts varies with art, artist, and work. Sometimes one aspect dominates to the virtual exclusion of the other two; compare Debussy's *La Mer*, Bach's *Goldberg's Variations*, and Charles Ives's *Fourth Symphony*, for instance; or a Durer watercolour, a Jackson Pollock painting, and a Soulages Lithograph. In other cases two or all three aspects, fused or in counterpoint, are almost equally prominent . . . The choice is up to the artist, and judgement up to the critic.[50]

The shift from realism to subjectivism in the case of visual art is particularly easy to comprehend precisely because it can be directly observed. But it can equally be heard in the history of music in the same period. From the representational works of the nineteenth century – including the occasional imitation of nature – to the piece *4'33''* by John Cage, a work summarised by Paul Griffiths in this way:

> It was only a small step [from *Music of Changes*] to make the outcome of a piece entirely a matter of chance, by liberalising the notation, and Cage took that step in his *4'33''* (1952). In this work, originally given by a solo pianist

but not unadaptable to other forces, there is no notated sound at all: the musicians remain silent, the piece 'consisting' of the sounds of the environment, and, like as not, those of the audience. Inevitably, *4′33″* was received as a joke, but there was a serious intention to it, or rather, in Cage's terms, a 'non-intention'.[51]

This 'collapse of the realist ambition' is comparable to the similar phenomenon in the visual arts in the same period. Donald Mitchell indeed, in *The Language of Modern Music*, regarded the coincidence of Picasso's 'Les Demoiselles d'Avignon' and Schoenberg's second string quartet having been produced in the same years, 1907–8, as being so remarkable, 'that one might almost suspect collusion!'[52] Accepting John Golding's judgment that 'Les Demoiselles' is 'the logical point to begin a history of Cubism',[53] he then commented on Schoenberg:

> Schoenberg's second string quartet . . . is no less of a logical point from which to embark upon a survey of the steps which led him subsequently to the development of the serial method (steps which comprised its development, indeed). The work, as Erwin Stein remarks, 'marks a turning point in Schoenberg's compositions. He had looked across the borders of a tonality governed by a central key . . .' In the finale of the quartet we encounter him outward bound from tonality, upon the verge of the 'dismissal of a system which had conditioned Western music since the seventeenth century'.[54]

But the shift from form to abstraction was not immediate. The shift to the serial method of composition still allowed the possibility of 'melodic regeneration'. Thus Mitchell could go on to ask what is still a critically realist question about Schoenberg: what is his music 'about'? 'Schoenberg's music is "about" its melody (I use the term here to include the whole thematic process). However "absolute" his music may be, the question "what is it about?" can always be put, and, in this "absolute" sense, receive a meaningful answer: "It is about these themes and their development." '[55]

In contrast Stockhausen could comment on his own work: 'Thus no recapitulation, no variation, no development. All that presupposes "formal procedures" – themes and motifs that are repeated, varied, developed, contrasted, worked out . . . All that I have abandoned since the first purely pointilliste works.'

Realism, Anti-Realism and Reliability

In all these different domains, and in these very different ways, we can trace the collapse of realist ambitions with their displacement by a recognition of the relativity, incompleteness and subjectivity of virtually all our judgments. It is not just in Einsteinian relativity (in fact in relation not only to quantum theories but to all physics Einstein remained a realist to the end of his life), nor simply in the shift to a participant universe: we can see it also in other major revolutions, in the recognition of cultural relativity in anthropology, in Gödel's theorem in mathematics, in conventionalism in the sociology of knowledge, in deconstructionism in literary criticism, in moral relativity and situation ethics in life, in the shift from tonality to atonality in music, in the move from form to abstraction in sculpture, in the advent of the absurd in the theatre, in the 'death of God' in theology.

All these in their different ways are acknowledgements of the provisionality, relativity and incompleteness of virtually all our judgments. William Tucker, in a book on modern sculpture, put the point very briefly when he was echoing the rallying cry of aestheticism, 'the autonomy of art': the artistic creation *had* to become an object in its right and on its own terms. If it is evaluated simply or mainly in terms of its correspondence to some other object (in nature, in what we take to be the case 'out there'), then the closer it corresponds, the less point there is for its existence:

As the sculpture-object approached the reality-object in form and intention, the gap between them dwindled to the point at which all reasons for making sculpture, and indeed art in general, seemed to disappear. This was the nature of the crisis that was experienced by advanced art in the 1920s, when most artists – including those who had been chiefly responsible in achieving the success of 'the object' in sculpture and painting, Brancusi and Picasso – seem to

60

have felt an impulse to move backwards or forwards violently. It was as though the position gained were incapable of steady development, but demanded, either the unconditional surrender of the conventions with which they had been warring (but on whose existence their art had depended), or counter-revolution.[57]

Are we then condemned to the same state, of living in a constant condition of counter-revolution? Yes, according to the antirealist conclusion drawn by Feyerabend in his anarchistic theory of knowledge. If realism were as dead as Cupitt declares, then that would be a correspondingly proper conclusion to draw about theology. But realism is *not* dead – except, maybe, in the forms of such obvious naivety that even to state them is to lapse, almost inevitably, into caricature – the form of realism which believes that there is nothing more complicated in knowing that something is the case than going out and 'taking a look' – and believing that the evidence of one's senses is privileged and incorrigible.[58]

The antirealism of the last hundred years has made naive empiricism untenable. Asked by Bryan Magee what, in retrospect, he regarded the main defects of logical positivism as having been, A. J. Ayer (one of its principal architects) replied, 'Well, I suppose the most important of the defetcs was that nearly all of it was false.'[59] The kind of critical realism which has replaced it accepts the incompleteness, provisionality, approximation and corrigibility of our judgments about virtually anything. It accepts as true that many of our ways of imagining or describing or thinking about what we take to be the case (whether of God or of the universe) will turn out to be incomplete and maybe wrong, in some or many respects, from another and later perspective: earth's proud empires fade away; so do its cosmologies, philosophies, anthropologies, psychologies, theologies, technologies and all the rest. *But* in all or most of these there can be irreversible gains, genuine and enduring achievements: not *everything* is swept away. Logical positivism, in its classical form, may have been 'mostly false', but no philosopher can any longer write philosophy as he might have attempted to do so before – without, that is, an entirely different and careful attention to language and sentences.[60] There are irreversible gains in understanding, argument and technology: 150 years ago we were travelling by stage-coach, now by train, bus, bike or car; but we do not have to reinvent the wheel each time. This is not to confuse such gains with progress. It is simply to observe that despite the incompleteness of human knowledge we can say and do many things with a confidence accumulated through time. And that is true also of what we say and do in relation to God.

So a really basic issue remains open: given that we cannot ever achieve full, complete or final accounts of anything very much, and certainly not of the universe, how does it come about that we nevertheless live in worlds of immense reliability? After all, we do, with great reliability, bump into what we take to be tables (conventional language), and fail to walk through walls; we succeed in falling down mountains when we miss the path; we know that if we fuse sodium benzenesulphonate with sodium hydroxide we will form (what we call) carbolic acid; we know that if we react coal with hydrogen at high pressure, at a fairly precise temperature, and usually in the presence of some such catalyst as cobalt molybdenum, we will end up producing oil; we know that occasionally a bridge falls down in Connecticut, an engine falls off a plane, and a chemical plant explodes; but in general they stay up, they stay on and they stay stable.

To say such things is to say, as briefly as possible, that we do live in highly reliable though no doubt dangerous and statistical worlds (of which, we have to accept, we know extremely little). How do we achieve different sorts of reliability if there is no limit set upon our language by what in reality occurs, in *some* distinction from our own construction or our own talk about it? Or, to put the point more sharply to Cupitt's position, how does it come about that some provisional, albeit incomplete, reliability can be discovered in virtually every other form of human reflection and enquiry but never apparently in theology? So far as science is concerned, the point is very often made in favour of critical realism, that if you move away from theory to the practice of science, it is extremely hard to find a practising scientist who does not act towards and upon his subject matter in a totally realistic way. It was a physicist, Mario Bunge, who put this point very forcibly, in answer to the question in an interview:

'In your view which way should physics go, i.e., what kind of theories should one attempt to build?' Bunge replied:

> As a physicist I couldn't care less which way fundamental physics goes just so long as it keeps going. In particular, I do not care whether physics remains basically probabilistic or else becomes even more radically stochastic (by replacing all extant parameters and dispersion-free variables by random variables) or, what seems unlikely, turns around and goes deterministic in the classical sense.[61]

But Bunge then went on to say what, as a *philosopher*, he *does* care about – and the first of those concerns is realistic, 'that physics remains physical – i.e., concerned with physical objects rather than with observers and their mental states.'

But in fact recent defences of critical realism have said that we need to be concerned about *both;* and that we need to draw the appropriate distinctions between both, rather than regarding them as competitors for an epistemological vote. Examples would be Michael Devitt, *Realism and Truth,* Ian Hacking, *Representing and Intervening,* Nancy Cartwright, *How the Laws of Physics Lie* (a beautifully ambiguous title which exactly catches the basic ambivalence). What these three examples have in common is that in different ways they distinguish the metaphysical, ontological issue of realism from any semantic issue. To that extent, they are reflecting Tarski's crucial recognition that what are true are sentences; to ascertain *how* sentences are related to what they purport to be about, truly or falsely, is a different undertaking. As Devitt put the point: 'The metaphysical issue of realism is the fundamental one in our theory of the largely impersonal world. Semantic issues arise in our theory of people (and their like) in their relations to that world.'[62]

Hacking and Cartwright are more concerned with the actual *practice* of science – how does it proceed, and what happens experimentally? But they end up with a comparable distinction. What they and other realists are maintaining is that there is some limit set over our ways of thinking which is not of our own construction; and that while it is indeed true that we cannot have any conception of reality which is not mediated by our concepts, it does not even remotely follow from that alone that there is no reality outside our concepts. That means that we can be thoroughly anti-realist in relation to theories (in other words, we can accept the limitations *of* language) while at the same time being unashamedly realist in the ways in which we live and act upon the world (which means that we can accept the limitations *on* language which the world imposes).

It is in this way, and evidently for these reasons, that Quine has come to regard himself as a relativist in relation to languages, and an absolutist in relation to knowledge, conceived not as certainty, but as 'true belief on strong evidence':

> There is indeed a clear and trivial sense in which truth, Tarski's, is relative to language. What are true are sentences, and a sentence of one language is . . . the gibberish of another. Relativism in this sense I can unabashedly own. At the same time there is an absolutism, a robust realism, that is part and parcel of my naturalism. Science itself, in a broad sense, and not some ulterior philosophy, is where judgement is properly passed, however fallibly, on questions of truth and reality. What is affirmed there, on the best available evidence, is affirmed as absolutely true.[63]

Superficially it might still be possible to regard this way of combining anti-realism (in relation to language) with realism (in relation to constraints on judgment) as improper, and to insist on a choice one way or the other – by declaring, for example, that 'realism is dead'. And certainly participants in the debate can interpret it competitively in that way. Thus in 1977 the revised and second edition came out of an Indiana symposium on *The Structure of Scientific Theories*. When the symposium met in 1969 it could record only uncertainty, 'in the midst of the disarray' in which the dominant position of logical empiricism in the philosophy of science was being challenged – and indeed, destroyed. But by 1977, when Suppe, the editor, looked back on what had happened in the intervening years, he could comment:

> Much has happened in the eight years since the symposium: (1) Positivistic philosophy of science has gone into near total eclipse; (2) the more extreme *Weltanschauungen*

64

views of Feyerabend, Hanson and Kuhn no longer are serious contenders for becoming a replacement analysis; and (3) philosophy of science is coalescing around a new movement or approach which espouses a hard-nosed metaphysical and epistemological realism that focuses much of its attention on 'rationality in the growth of scientific knowledge' and proceeds by the examination of historical and contemporary examples of actual scientific practice.[64]

Yet it was in exactly that same year, 1977, that Barnes published his *Interests and the Growth of Knowledge;* and he saw the tide flowing very strongly in *his* direction. Having drawn the contrast between a contemplative account of knowledge (one which 'assumes that . . . individuals intrude minimally between reality and its representation; they apprehend reality *passively*, and, as it were, let it speak for itself')[65] and an instrumentalist or conventionalist account (one in which 'all knowledge is primarily instrumental . . . knowledge cannot be understood as more than the product of men operating in terms of an interest in prediction and control shaped and particularised by the specifics of their situations'),[66] he then commented:

> In sociology, the contemplative account has always coexisted with a sharply contrasted alternative, and at the present time it is the latter toward which the general trend is moving. Increasingly, knowledge is being treated as essentially social, as a part of the culture which is transmitted from generation to generation, and as something which is actively developed and modified in response to practical contingencies.[67]

But in the account of the matter which is being argued – and reported – here, there is a truth in *both* these accounts which can – and indeed must – be held in conjunction. It is therefore important to be clear what they both maintain in common. On the one hand, both accept that there cannot be any representation of how the world may be, which is not embedded in theory. So to give an example of the acceptance of this on the realist side: an extreme form of realism is 'fallibilistic absolutism' – the view that we achieve, progressively, representations of the universe which 'portray it ever

65

more nearly as it is, not as it appears from some particular vantage point.'[68] Jardine (from whom that quotation comes) postulates a human inquiry series, constantly open to correction, which does not indeed explain all aspects of the experience of all possible sentient beings, but which holds simply that there cannot be any such aspect which will forever resist explanation.[69] The human inquiry series, by its corrigibility from without, moves in that direction, and in that sense can be defended as 'a fallibilist absolutism, an absolutism which claims objective progress for the natural sciences whilst abandoning all hope of attainment of completeness or certainty'.[70]

All that is in considerable contrast to Feyerabend, Kuhn and Barnes. Nevertheless Jardine accepts the approximate and corrigible nature of our accounts, and also the inescapable primacy of theory for such accounts to be given:

> To attempt to specify absolutely a relation of correspondence between the world and representations of the world is futile. This view is, I think, inescapable. If absolutism is to be rendered intelligible we must, at the outset, be content with the notion of truth (and its cognates, reference, consistency, equivalence, etc.) from the standpoint of a representation of the world, that is, a theory.[71]

So both sides, realist and anti-realist, accept that virtually all our accounts of anything, even of something as superficially obvious as the universe, are approximate, corrigible, incomplete and provisional. But on the other side, there are few anti-realists (giving conventionalist or instrumentalist accounts of knowledge) who do not accept that there are what Barnes calls 'primitive causes in reality':

> Everything of naturalistic significance would indicate that there is indeed one world, one reality, 'out there', the source of our perceptions if not their total determinant, the cause of our expectations being fulfilled or disappointed, of our endeavours succeeding or being frustrated. But this reality should not be identified with any linguistic account of it, or, needless to say, with any way of perceiving it, or pictorial representation of it. Reality is the source of *primitive causes*, which, having been pre-processed by our perceptual apparatus, produce changes in our knowledge and the verbal

66

representations of it which we possess. All cultures relate symmetrically to this reality. Men in all cultures are capable of making reasonable responses to the causal inputs they receive from reality – that is, are capable of learning. That the structure of our verbal knowledge does not thereby necessarily converge upon a single form, isomorphous with what is real, should not surprise us. Why ever should we expect this to be a property of our linguistic and cognitive capabilities?[72]

The unity of these accounts lies in the recognition of instantiation – of instantiating data – data which constrain and set a limit on our judgments. It is not controversial between these two sides that a disturbance *'in stat'* (in the Latin), 'stands into', instantiates itself in our awareness as a datum – hence instantiating data. Nor is it controversial that we then decode that disturbance according to the contexts in which we are, and the theories or the pictures that are available to us. They may be the naive pictures of common sense, which are undoubtedly provisional, corrigible and incomplete, but nevertheless extremely reliable for most purposes; or in more specialised circumstances they may be the theories of physics, or chemistry, or religion, or the more personal and individual pictures of a poet or an artist. None of these accounts can capture the whole meaning of the instantiating data or the totality of what they might signify nor, if they purport to be descriptive, can they ever be immune from corrigibility. But they are evoked by those instantiations, and they are constrained and delimited by them. They are not wholly random or arbitrary.

Clearly it is possible, as we have just seen, for art to protest against constraint; but that is simply one different way of relating to instantiation – and it may produce highly private interpretations. But the reason why art, science, religion, poetry do not *have* to become totally private lies in the fact that what the American critic Giles Gunn calls 'interpretation of otherness' is not random or arbitrary.[73] It is constrained by data, made public through extensive intersubjective networks of report and interpretation – as much, incidentally, in the case of God as of the universe. Certainly it is possible for our judgments to be idiosyncratic and private, but they do not have to be: if I hold up a round metallic object and say, 'what is it?' you and others may well answer '10p'. That judgment is socially and instrumentally constructed: it is a convention that this chunked-up alloy replaces direct barter of sheep and goats; it is a linguistic convention that we now call it 10p and no longer a florin; but equally, that judgment has been constrained and delimited – controlled into its outcome – by the regularity of its instantiation: 10p pieces are not round today and square tomorrow.

In general, where there is sufficient regularity of instantiation, then a limit is set on our language and judgment, even though, to reiterate the point, we can never fully, finally or exhaustively say all there is to be said about this particular datum, this particular event, this particular appearance. We do not know what it really *is*, but realistically we are constrained into a public language about its appearance and use. It follows that we will all remain approximately wrong about what is the case, so long as our descriptions remain incomplete – which they will.

Nevertheless it follows also that reliability, to be worth having, does not have to reach a degree of absolute certainty. Very different degrees and kinds of reliability are attained (and are found to *be* reliable) in an immense variety of different enterprises; and they emerge in such things as science, history, commonsense, sociology, the administration of justice, marriage, economics, orienteering, doing the pools; whereas in some enterprises (for example, the popular, and perhaps all, forms of astrology) there is no reliability at all. Where the sciences are concerned the constant probing and testing of reliability, generation by generation, is what has made them also 'well-winnowed traditions' (see p. 7): the sciences are well-winnowed traditions of great reliability, while still remaining provisional, corrigible and incomplete. They can *never* give a final account of 'how the universe really is'. That will always lie beyond us. But they can give accounts which are highly reliable for particular purposes, and they can eliminate some other accounts as failing in coherence or correspondence or reference or reliability or usefulness or validity – or whatever else may be involved in truth.

That scientific knowledge is so profoundly *corrigible* is directly contrary to the popular assumption that it is the only valid way of knowing anything. The corrigibility of science can lead – and in fact has led – to massive corrections of its own past or present: the sequence from the Newtonian absolutes of space and time, to Einstein and relativity, to Bohr and quantum mechanics, is an instructive example of this process. It also illustrates the vital point that Newton did not suddenly become 'wrong' overnight. The older theory remains valid enough (in the kind of time and space in which human beings live) for it to be highly reliable for many practical purposes. The operational success of satellites and space probes is a witness to the enduring validity of Newton's laws, even though in other ways his conception of the physical universe has been superseded by the (incomplete) insights of quantum mechanics.[74]

Nevertheless some pictures, proposals and imaginings about the universe have been discarded completely, although for generations they seemed secure and necessary. Spissitude, phlogiston, caloric and ether were all, in their time, believed to have real existence. They were thought necessary, in order to explain processes such as combustion and the propagation of light. Yet all of them have had to be rejected as non-existent: the unfamiliarity of the terms shows how completely they have been abandoned. Nevertheless for centuries the instantiating data seemed to demand the inference of ether: how else could sound and light propagate as waves? 'All space', wrote Newton, 'is permeated by an elastic medium or aether, which is capable of propagating vibrations of sound, only with far greater velocity.' We have already seen (pp. 46–7) how hard it was to recognise the non-existence of the ether.

Similarly the persistent datum – that matter appears to be inert, and yet that one object moves another – seemed to Henry More to require an inherent and additional power which he called 'spissitude'. Again the instantiating data of combustion seemed to require the inference of phlogiston, since something, surely, is expelled from a burning entity. And even when the role of oxygen was identified and phlogiston was shown to be empty of reference, there was still the datum of heat – persistent, consistent and reliable in its instantiation: but what account to give of it? Even Lavoisier inferred 'caloric' as a substance. In his list of elements in

1789 'calorique' appears as one of the *'substances simples qui appartiennent aux trois règnes et qu'on peut regarder comme les élémens des corps'*.

It would be easy to multiply examples of the corrigibility of science: there was a time when the earth was static and somewhere near the centre of the universe; when insects and mice, fish and frogs were spontaneously generated from decaying matter; when the blood flowed in two systems, the venous and the arterial, passing from one to the other through invisible pores in the septum of the heart, and through anastomoses, or minute openings, between the veins and the arteries. And the process of correction continues. It is only as recently as 1906 that Robert Peary on his way to the North Pole stood on Cape Thomas Hubbard and saw to the northwest, at a distance of what he took to be 120 miles, a new land of hills and valleys and snow-covered mountains. But he had reached the limit of his supplies. He wrote later: 'My heart leaped the intervening miles of ice as I looked longingly at this land and in fancy as the first explorer I trod its shores and climbed its summits, even though I knew that that pleasure could only be for another in another season.'[75]

That other turned out to be D. B. MacMillan, who set out to explore what had become known, in the interim, as 'Crocker Land'; and as he approached he saw exactly the same array of hills and mountains spreading out over 120° of the horizon before him. But as he got closer than this with his expedition the whole of Crocker Land disappeared. It turned out to be an instance of what is known as Fata Morgana (so-called after the fairy Morgan, the sister of King Arthur, who had the magic power of creating castles in the air). In other words it is a spectacular example of a mirage – of a consequence, that is, of particular atmospheric conditions in which the temperature gradient near the inflection point in the temperature profile is slightly smaller than it is for a three-image mirage, and in which therefore the apparent shape of the water's surface does not fold over, but rises up and forms a wall. Since light reaches the eye in a distorted wave front, the surface of the apparent object cannot be reported uniformly but only in variations of light and shade. It is then easy to 'see' castles in the air, or non-existent countries to be explored.

Our languages here, whether we are using the terms of mythology or optics, are conventional, and they surely draw attention to the corrigibility of our judgments. Crocker Land is a particularly good example of the ways in which the eye can be deceived. But the conclusion to be drawn from the deceived eye is not that we are therefore so deceived about everything that anything might be true, or that nothing can ever be true; but rather that we have sufficient security in our collectively experienced world to distinguish the relative degrees of deceipt. Quinton put the point briefly: 'The argument from illusion draws attention to the necessary truth that we know, anyway, what appears epistemically to be the case.'[76]

What, then, are we to say of that illusion of whose future Freud wrote so pessimistically fifty or so years ago – in other words, of religion? We have already seen that, whatever else they are, religions are organised systems for the protection of information, in which resources are made available to individuals and groups for the constraint and construction of their lives. What those resources are and how we relate to them are very differently described in different religions – and in very approximate languages. However, in general, the environment in which a religious imagination lives and from which it derives significant constraint is a great deal more extensive than the environment in which, say, a physicist's imagination – *qua* physics – is operating. That is so because the constraints which are believed to be derived from (for example) God are not discerned simply in those modes of attention which adjudicate on the structure of an atom or the composition of a star. They may overlap as subject matter for some people; but in general the more important point is that there are idiosyncratic ways of attending to the possibility of God, ways which are what they are, and are not like anything else; and these ways of attending have been tested, changed, corrected, confirmed, intersubjectively through long centuries of accumulated consequence and experience – just as, comparably, there are idiosyncratic ways of attending as a scientist to the possibility of the universe, which have also been tested, corrected, confirmed and changed in their own way; so that both the sciences and religions are idiosyncratically (in relation to their own subject-matters) well-winnowed traditions: both modes of attentiveness have been evoked, and have become what they are, by sufficient persistence in the instantiating data. The data are not identical nor are the ways of attending to them. But in both cases, the crucial fact remains that there is sufficient persistence and consistency in the data for there to be built up, intersubjectively and collectively, provisional but often extremely reliable pictures and theories of what we are entitled to infer to be the case about those data, if they have given rise to those sorts of experiences.

It was for these reasons, and along this kind of route, that Husserl (the founding father of phenomenology and also, perhaps more memorably, of modern existentialism) came to believe, against his initial perception, that questions of reality and ontology are unavoidable.[77] Initially he had hoped to by-pass the perennial, but unresolved, argument between solipsism and realism. He began with a move even more radical than that of Descartes (the only thing of which I can be indubitably certain is that I think, therefore I, at least am), by arguing that I cannot in fact be certain of anything except 'appearances in consciousness'. I certainly cannot adjudicate on what gives rise to those appearances, nor on whether they 'exist' outside my own consciousness of them. However, that issue (the traditional one of solipsism vs. realism) becomes irrelevant when I become aware of appearances in my consciousness of unmistakable persistence and regularity (conventionally known as people) which appear in the particular manner of communicating *with* me, thereby marking off *other* appearances in correspondingly persistent and regular ways – and these, too, can be coded in different languages, as (for example) chairs and tables, stars and stones. Such appearances, which we call 'people', Husserl called 'walking object indices', through which are built up, intersubjectively, reliable (though always approximate) accounts of appearances in consciousness.

But in so far as these *are* reliable and persistent and help to organise the function of an individual in ways appropriate to particular contexts (which is not to say that individuals cannot behave inappropriately; but that simply makes the same point in reverse), so Husserl felt entitled to infer a sufficient existence in reality to account for the 'appearances in consciousness' appearing with the sort of persistence and reliability that they do. Clearly the appearances and the nature of their persistence and reliability differ greatly, and Husserl was prepared to accept regional ontologies: or to put it the other way round, he was only prepared to return that degree of reality to the world which the nature of the appearances in question seem to demand or allow. As Robert Tragesser has summarised the point:

> Even brief reflection reveals an enormous variety of objects of thought: trees, stars, personalities, civilisations, poems, numbers, infinite sets, demons, gods, emotions, acts of violence and love, persons alive and dead, pi mesons . . . Many seem to require very different means of being apprehended and thought about. It is not only their diversity which must be accounted for, but the very nature of the development of thought, the irregular shifts of conceptual background, which themselves contribute to the proliferation of apparent entities.[78]

So the question that Husserl was asking was this: what may, and sometimes what must, we infer as a sufficient ground in reality (in other words, sufficient ontological ground) for those persistent reliabilities to obtain which do obtain (given that we cannot talk completely or incorrigibly about them)? What is implied by a regional ontology is that questions of existence cannot be resolved in the abstract, but only by returning that degree of reality to the instantiating data which the (diachronic – that is, well-winnowed) intersubjective accounts of the data seem to demand. In that way he returned a high degree of reality to such intersubjective regional domains of enquiry and discourse as mathematics, natural science and commonsense.

At the very end of his life Husserl began to realise that a corresponding degree of reality must be returned to God, since theology, in so far as it is parasitic on experience (as basically it is), is equally well-winnowed and tested through time – though in a regionally different way. Thus the correspondence, in relation to other inferential systems, is not in the least exact not only because the instantiating data in the case of theology (while they may be mediated in and through the universe) are not identical with the universe; but also, more prosaically, because the religious systems associated with the process of theology frequently claim to be incorrigible in so far as they are constrained by revelation. But that does not affect the immediate point that theistic religions and theology are a consequence of instantiating data, of an idiosyncratic kind (since otherwise theology would have merged with some other kind of inquiry long ago); and that in the case of God, as in other persistent and well-winnowed cases, we are entitled to infer a realistic counterpart, by way of constraint, over against those approximate languages which we use, and those corrigible pictures which we construct. In the case of God, as of the universe, there appears to be 'a responsive Otherness', different though the modes of attentiveness and interaction are in each case.

It follows immediately that there is no necessity to abandon critically realist languages about God. Indeed, exactly the reverse, it is hard to see what other language could possibly be used, given the persistence and consistency in the data. It is true that God is not an object *like* a universe, or an object *in* a universe, to be explored and investigated by apparatus and experiments. But it is equally true that God does not depend for his existence or nature on our opinions or concepts about him, and that his reality does set limits on our language about him. Although (see p. 63) we cannot have any apprehension of God which is not mediated by our concepts, it does not follow that there is no reality in the case of God apart from our concepts. And that is not in the least affected by the fact that our concepts, pictures and imaginings about God, as about anything else, are necessarily incomplete, provisional, approximate and corrigible.

That last point is so important that it can be put more sharply: if all our pictures and imaginings, even of something as relatively obvious as the observable universe, are necessarily incomplete and corrigible, we should not be upset or alarmed if the same is true in theology. A real cause for alarm would be if theology *could* provide a complete and realistic representation of God, because any such literally accurate 'model' of God would be an idol.

It is true that scientists as much as theologians offer 'models' of what they take or believe to be real, to help their own understanding; but they do not use the term in its colloquial, everyday sense. A model, in everyday language, is either someone exhibiting clothes for someone else to wear, or it is a reproduction of some real object on a different scale: either smaller, like a toy train or an architect's model of a proposed building, or larger, like the complex models of molecules in a chemistry laboratory. But our imaginings of the universe – let alone of God – are not like that. They are more like representations (literally, 're-presentations') of selected aspects of reality, which do not pretend to be models in the everyday sense. A good example would be the different ways in which it is possible to draw maps of the same area of ground. An ordnance survey map re-presents territory with conventional signs, and it enables us to recognise where we are and how to proceed – that is if we are able to 'read a map'. But it certainly does not portray the territory as a realist painter might have done, or even as correspondently as an aerial photograph. An Underground map is even less related to the actual topography of the experience of walking around London; but it re-presents information about that reality which enables particular procedures (of catching trains, or of getting from Euston to Victoria) in relation to it.

Similarly most maps of the world transform the dimensions of a sphere on to the one dimension of the page of an atlas by means of the Mercator projection. But the Peters projection, adopted by the Brandt Report, represents territory by a decimal degree network which reduces the Eurocentric emphasis of the Mercator projection. Even more extreme is the world map produced by John Fagg, which represents each territory according to its GNP, and which therefore represents to the eye the distribution of poverty and wealth, not some direct model of the ground as it is.

Does this mean that we can invent any map we want to? Yes, in fiction: Tolkien's Middle Earth, Bunyan's Pilgrim's Progress; but not in geography because there are limits set upon our language or map-drawing by what is really the case, no matter how corrigible and incomplete our maps may be. If maps have to be evaluated in terms of their exact correspondence to the ground they are attempting to describe, then certainly we can say that realism is dead. But if we regard the ground, independently of our map-making activities, as setting a limit on our languages (whether pictorial or other-

75

wise), then we have to say that a critical realism is necessary for human community and reason – and for truth. It means inevitably (and this is so for theology as much as for geography or the natural sciences) that there will have to be many complementary ways of attending to the same data. Clerk Maxwell (of the Maxwell-Boltzmann 'disturbance', p. 47) once wrote: 'Scientific truth should be presented in different forms, and should be regarded as equally scientific, whether it appears in the robust form and vivid colouring of a physical illustration, or in the tenuity and paleness of a symbolic expression.'[79] Pictures are incomplete; but (or perhaps 'and for that reason') they can nevertheless reinforce and complement each other.

Conversely there is a further implication, that all theological pictures, propositions and imaginings carry with them the possibility of being defective or even wrong. We should not be surprised or alarmed that this is so. Some of the pictures of God that have been imagined in the past may come to be discarded, even though, like the scientific pictures of caloric and the ether (p. 69), they have long seemed to be realistic and have served many generations faithfully as ways of interacting with God. Thus, for example, it is simply not the case that hell is a place located somewhere immediately beneath our feet, or that God sits literally on a throne in a golden city somewhere above our heads. It is simply not the case that the creation of the world began at six o'clock in the evening of 22 October in the year 4004 BC, and took 144 hours to complete.

But the fact that the theological imagination is corrigible, and that we can trace the history of particular conceptual episodes (even, in some instances, to the decline and fall of their empire) does *not* mean that that imagination is not 'about' some reality independent of itself. There is a distinction between saying that our judgments are corrigible, approximate and no doubt frequently wrong, and saying that we cannot rely on anything. If you are ill and call in a doctor you have to accept that his judgments about your illness may be mistaken – in other words they are corrigible and incomplete. But you would be foolish for that reason to regard his as unreliable; for he lives at the end (up to this point) of a well-winnowed tradition of medical knowledge – incomplete though that necessarily is – and there is a *limit* set on his judgment, diagnosis and theories by what is actually happening in the disease of your body.

The distinction is clear: 'God' is not a word or set of pictures which we use as part of our approximate attempts to describe something else – some way of experiencing the universe or the depth of our relations with each other. Rather, what God truly is, is what constrains and sets a limit on our approximate language about him – just as what is, in the case of the universe, constrains and sets a limit on our approximate (and quite different) language about it. In neither case can those languages be descriptively complete. But the life and experience of people, on which theology depends, make it clear that although in our present condition we see through a glass darkly, we do at least begin to see; and it establishes reliably the belief that what shall be in the End will not end, but will make complete what is here known only in part.

So if we ask why theology should think, fundamentally, that it has a necessity to speak, the answer has to be, basically, because it is a consequence of the long and well-winnowed experience of women and men that there is One who makes a demand upon them which is more like the demand of a person than that of an impersonal object, to whom they respond in awe, worship, love, prayer, contemplation, adoration – and in action, in acting in the world in ways that have him as their deepest and most abiding resource. The objectivity of that demand is believed to issue, at an extreme, in revelation. Yet even here – and perhaps most of all here, in relation to revelation and scripture – we need to remember that no language, not even the language of scripture, can supply a complete, final and exhaustive description of what God is, in his own nature. That is why all accounts of God, in all religions, end up sooner or later by saying, much as Samuel Johnson said of Milton's religion, 'We know rather what he was not, than what he was.'[80] So religions inevitably end up in the *via negativa* of Christianity, the *En Soph* of Judaism, the *bila kaif* of Islam, the *neti neti* of Hinduism (not this not this), the *ik onkar* of Sikhism.

In that limited sense there is a resemblance between our response to the universe and our response to God. What we take to be the universe makes demands upon us in particular and consistent ways, to which we can respond, if we choose to, in the ways appropriate to those demands. What we take to be God makes its demands upon us likewise in particular and consistent ways, to which again we can respond, if we wish to, in the ways appropriate to those demands; and what those 'ways of attending' are, forms a part of the subject matter of the study of religion. Clearly, to repeat the point made earlier, they are different from those modes of attention which adjudicate on the structure of the atom or the composition of a star; but that simply means that there *are* idiosyncratic ways of attending to the possibility of God – ways which are what they are, and are not identical with anything else, because the instantiations which evoke them are distinctive.

The nature of those instantiations which evoke the later reflective language about God are extremely diverse. The possibility of God may instantiate itself through the data of the universe apprehended in a particular way – as being derived, for example, from the unproduced Producer of all that is; or it may be in the perception of my neighbour making a demand on myself as the occasion of love transcending interest; or in the recognition of what is acting by way of constraint on lives made admirable by grace; or in the more direct apprehension of God in worship, meditation, prayer, contemplation, in which the instantiation may be of such a kind that it is more like being apprehended than apprehending; or it may be in the acceptance of the self-revealing of God through particular words and actions; or in the reception of information (of disturbance and change in the recipient) through those protected channels of communication to which Christians refer as sacraments; or in the demand of beauty or of meaning when kingfishers catch fire,[81] or rooks shake feathers in the rain.[82] The point is put eloquently by that same George Moore of the argument with McFee (p. 38), in Tom Stoppard's *Jumpers:*

How does one know what it is one believes when it's so difficult to know what it is one knows? I don't claim to *know* that God exists, I only claim that he does without my knowing it, and while I claim as much I do not claim to know as much; indeed I cannot know and God knows I cannot. (*Pause.*) And yet I tell you that, now and again, not necessarily in the contemplation of rainbows or new-born babes, nor in extremities of pain or joy, but more probably ambushed by some quite trivial moment – say the exchange of signals between two long-distance lorry-drivers in the black sleet of a god-awful night on the old A1 – then in that dip-flash, dip-flash of headlights in the rain that seems to affirm some common ground that is not animal and not long-distance lorry-driving – then I tell you I *know*.[83]

Moore then pulls himself up in some embarrassment ('I sound like a joke vicar') and pursues the argument in directions that McFee and others would doubtless not follow. But the issue of inference from instantiation is very clearly put.

That passage also makes the point, indirectly, that the inference does not *have* to be theistic. But in many cases it may be: the instantiating data which demand the inference of God are immensely diverse. We are not immune from error in identifying them, nor in attempting to say something about them, nor in describing what we infer as a sufficient and necessary ground to account for them. But we are still entitled to ask, in this case (of God) as we did in the other (of the universe), about *what* are we approximately wrong? We are entitled to return that degree of reality to a supposed counter-part to our experience as is demanded by the nature of that experience, and by the persistence and consistency of the data as it is shared intersubjectively through space and time. It is in this way, since the persistence and consistency of the data are so very impressive in the case of God, that we are entitled (indeed, in terms of truth are required) to reject the view that realism is dead, and to accept that we can use a critically realist language of God. No one doubts that it must be approximate. But to repeat the point: while it is true that we cannot have any conception of this reality which is not mediated by our concepts, it does not even remotely follow from that alone that there is no reality outside our concepts.

That is why it is trivial to say that 'religion is made by men for men' (p. 41), and that science, religion and God are human inventions. Of course they are. Everything is a human invention in language. But the Latin word *invenio* means 'I come into'. So the issue is whether there are *data*, given things, into which we come as we explore and extend the environments in which we live and move and have our being, which do not depend for their existence or nature on our opinion. To say that something is 'invented' is not necessarily to say that it is somehow less than real.

However, the fact still remains that there is that other sense of invented – of making something up that is not truly the case. A fiction (in the Latin root) is 'a deception'; and that is exactly what strongly reductionist accounts of believing in God (like those of Marx or Freud or sociobiology or genetic programmes) continue to say – that humans invent God in that fictional sense, because they need that fiction. If those accounts are successful, then surely we still have to conclude that we do not need the reality of God in order to account for believing in God. The case for a critically realistic language in relation to God may be in principle defensible; but if in practice people believe for more fundamental reasons in their own nature, or in society, then perhaps it will still be the case that language about 'God' is really (realistically) language about ourselves. Whether that is so is the question still to be considered.

3

Why Believe in God?

We are, it seems clear, compelled to accept that all our descriptive languages, even about something as relatively obvious as the universe, are approximate, incomplete, corrigible and frequently wrong. However, that does not mean there is no limit set upon our languages by what is really the case, even though what we say about that reality is always provisional and incomplete. If that is so in the case of what we take to be the universe, it can, in principle, be so of what we take to be God. However, from the fact that, logically, whatever is the case in the case of God would indeed set a limit on our language, it does not follow from that alone that there is anything that is the case, independently of ourselves, in the case of God: the fact that something may logically be so, does not entail that it is so. We are still entitled to ask the question, why then believe in God? To which the only possible answer can be – why indeed? The realities of evil and suffering will surely rule out for many the possibility of reconciling experience with the existence of God. 'How are atheists produced?' asked Bernard Shaw:

> In probably nine cases out of ten, what happens is something like this. A beloved wife or husband or child or sweetheart is gnawed to death by cancer, stultified by epilepsy, struck dumb and helpless by apoplexy, or strangled by croup or diptheria; and the looker-on, after praying vainly to God to refrain from such horrible and wanton cruelty, indignantly repudiates faith in the divine monster, and becomes not merely indifferent and sceptical, but fiercely and actively hostile to religion. What was at the back of it in nine cases out of ten was the horror of a God who was not only the God of honour, of love, and of light,

but also the God of epilepsy, of cancer, of smallpox, of madness, of war, of poverty, of tyranny: in short, of the huge burden of pain and evil under which the world has always groaned and is still groaning more pitifully than ever. In vain did the orthodox attempt to propitiate the agnostics by throwing over the imaginary hell of everlasting brimstone: they could not throw over the real hell which was flaming all around them. And so, as Nietzsche put it, the news went round that God was dead.[1]

That hostility may then be very powerfully reinforced by the accumulating history of wicked and evil deeds which have been done specifically in the name of God, and often with an appeal for his blessing on them. Martin Gardner wrote recently:

There is a famous statement by Augustine: If you love God you may do as you please. Alas, it is not so simple. The Spanish inquisitors loved God. The Christians who burned witches loved God. Promoters of the Children's Crusade loved God. John Calvin loved God when he allowed Servetus to be burned at the stake. Martin Luther loved God when he proposed driving Jews out of Germany. Jephthah loved God when he killed his daughter. Abraham loved God when he was willing to murder his son. Moses loved God when he ordered his soldiers to kill the old women and the male children of the Midianites, but to keep the virgin girls for themselves. In the bloody wars between Christians and Muslims, between Protestants and Catholics, all sides loved God.

Out of tens of thousands of horror stories about atrocities committed by those who loved God, I select one small example from the fifth-century Christianity. The world's first great woman mathematician, and the last great Neo-Platonist, was Hypatia. She was said to have been as beautiful as she was intelligent. Because she refused to become a Christian, a fanatical mob, inflamed by the Bishop of Alexandria (later canonized as Saint Cyril), seized her as she left a carriage, stripped her naked, scraped off her flesh with sharpened oyster shells, and burned her body. Charles Kingsley's novel *Hypatia* retells the grim story. One longs to be able to read Hypatia's many treatises on mathematics and philosophy, but they were all destroyed by Allah-loving Muslims when they burned the library at Alexandria. Why did they do this? Because, they said, if the books contained anything in the Koran they were not needed, and if they contained anything not in the Koran then they should not be read.[2]

It is irrelevant to the main issue to question whether the details of that history, or of its interpretation, are correct. No doubt there are other things that might be said. Far more important – and this was our point of departure – is to recognise the capacity of religious systems to foster violent and destructive behaviours. The Jews, with their characteristically ironic humour (one of the great saving graces of religion) tell a story of a sabbath service in nineteenth-century Poland. The doors of the holy sanctuary were open and the Ark of the Covenant had been unveiled. The rabbi was nodding in a chair on one side of the raised platform and the cantor was standing on the other side, chanting the day's words from the Holy Book. The men in the congregation, in their broad hats and prayer shawls, were bobbing their heads as they sat, murmuring the appropriate invocations at the name of God. The women, in their wigs and shawls and black dresses, were in the balcony, peering from the lattice that shielded them from the view of the men so that there should be no distraction in the holy service. Everything was as it had always been, so far as anyone knew, from the beginning of time. Suddenly the doors of the synagogue were thrown open and a man rushed down the centre aisle. He was coatless, hatless, wearing the rough clothes of a workman. His face was flushed, his hair was wild, his eyes were blazing. He turned to the congregation and shouted: 'You fools, you clods, you sheep! You worse than sheep, because sheep at least have shepherds who guide them to food and keep them safe from harm. All *your* shepherds can do' – pointing with a sneer at the rabbi and the cantor – 'is serve the wolves who feed on you. They teach you only how to suffer in silence while you live in fear and degradation and poverty. Week after week, year after year, you waste your lives chasing the hopeless dreams of the dead past, worshipping a thing that does not exist, when you could be out in the great world, learning the ways of nature unlocking the secrets of the universe, and using what you learn to build a world of peace and plenty. If I am wrong, may your supposed God in his supposed heaven tell me so!' And as he said these words, there came a great roar of thunder. The roof of the synagogue split open, lightning filled the sky. And the voice of God was heard, saying: 'You know, he's absolutely right!'[3]

There is no need to multiply examples. Given the strength of the case against God, why nevertheless would anyone still believe? Why indeed believe in God? And unlike most of the questions we ask, particularly in universities, that one can be answered very directly. Indeed, strangely, we can answer it in a single phrase: why believe in God? Because we have to. We are compelled into belief by necessity. Also strangely, that answer can be given with equal conviction by both atheists and believers. Both of them can answer that same question in the same way, by replying, Because we have to. They then, of course, immediately divide (or at least appear to divide), because they then supply entirely different lists of what those necessities are – of what it actually is that is compelling some people into believing in God. So we have to ask the question, what kinds of necessity, controlling people into believing in God, are being specified?

Reductionism and the Elimination of God

On the one side there is a list of necessities or compulsions which is strongly reductionist. That is to say, it suggests reasons why people believe in God which do not require the reality of God, or the existence of God, in order to account for that belief. The reasons why people believe in God are to be found here, within society, within our own nature, within our own frailties, or neuroses, or despair. Strongly reductionist accounts argue that the reasons why people believe in God are not because God is there to be believed in, but because we need to believe for many different reasons – because we have to. What reasons? Most of these are so familiar that there is no need to give an elaborate account of them. But by way of example (or rather, by way of six examples), why do people believe in God? Because, first, the image of God (particularly of God as judge who will reward or punish people after death) is so effective as an instrument of social control and stability that operators of human societies use and have used 'God' as a means of protecting their own privileges as long as they can get away with it. The argument is one of the oldest there is. Polybius was referring to it as ancient in about 125 BCE:

> Since the masses of the people are inconstant, full of unruly desires, passionate and reckless of consequence, they must be filled with fears to keep them in order. The ancients did well, therefore, to invent the gods and the belief in punishment after death. It is rather the moderns who seek to extirpate such beliefs who are to be accused of folly.[4]

This first example of a reductionist account (the cultivation of belief in God as a means of social control, manipulation and exploitation) is particularly associated with Marx. He at least appreciated that religion is the valve in the pressure cooker which allows the steam to get out into the kitchen. 'Religious distress is at the same time the expression of real distress and a protest against real distress. Religion is the sigh of the oppressed creature, it is the heart of a heartless world, just as it is the spirit of a spiritless situation. It is the opiate of the people.'[5]

Why then do people believe in God? Because they seek relief from their real distress in the wrong places. So we come to a second example. We are compelled into belief by psychological necessities within us. These are the necessities which arise when we cannot face the fact that our brief moment of life ends in oblivion, and that the universe is indifferent to us – or if it is not, it is largely hostile. The necessities which drive us into belief in God are not outside us, in the organisation of society to perpetuate alienation and class division. They are inside us, in our own psychology. We cannot face the futility of this world, so we construct a compensation outside, somewhere else, in an imaginary world: we project outside us some figures who *will* look after us, father gods and mother goddesses; and we construct these figures from the most profound but prelinguistic experience available to us, the experience of utter dependency in infancy. That has an immense bonus for us, because once we have projected a compensatory world 'out there', it enables us to resolve real conflicts (for example, oedipal conflicts) by transferring them into that imaginary world – and that *is* a bonus, because it means that you do not have to have murder and incest every time you come down to breakfast.

That summary of Freud is so brief that it is virtually a parody, but it is familiar anyway. What is important is that this, in a more general way, is probably the most widely-held view of why believers believe: it is because they cannot face their immediate neuroses and their eventual extinction and oblivion. In the succinct summary of Ambrose Bierce's *Devil's Dictionary*: 'Extinction: noun – the raw material out of which theology created the future state.' Freud's wilder speculations on the origins of religion have themselves gone away into well-deserved oblivion (since they bear no relation to such data as have survived), but in the years that have passed since *Totem and Taboo* and *Moses and Monotheism*, his basic proposal has received powerful reinforcement, that people believe in God because of underlying necessities in their psychological make-up; and the range of this kind of analysis is now so extreme that it can legitimately be counted as a third example of answering the question, 'Why do we believe?' with the answer, Because we have to.

In fact, there is a tangle of different proposals here, but in general they concentrate on early experience, which runs from pre-birth through infancy. One such account arises from the current brain research which attempts to map the ways in which particular structures in the brain (and the neural operators on them) are 'laid down' from genetic programmes – in other words they are genetically programmed and laid down in the brain in such a way that they prepare us for particular behaviours. Some of these are so obvious that they are not in the least controversial: we are prepared in advance for sucking on our mother's breast, for languages, for sexual behaviours, and so on: perhaps also we are prepared for God – prepared by this biogenetic structuralism for events and experiences in the brain which have seemed to require the inference of God.[6] If so, the slogan on the placard will no longer read 'Prepare to meet thy God'; it will read 'Prepared to meet thy God'. Jung's racial memory and recurrence of symbols would be another example in this category, but Jung was obviously

86

speaking in pre-genetic and imprecise language, of a more romantic kind.

However, Jung's intuitive anticipation of what the genes may well enable, is a reminder that not all these accounts of 'programmes of the brain' or of psychological necessity are strongly reductionist (meaning by 'strongly reductionist' accounts that do not require the existence of God to account for belief in God). Some of these accounts may even seem to require the existence of God (the reality of God) to account for the sort of nature that they have – a point which will be taken up at the end of this chapter. So psychological constraint or necessity is not unequivocally reductionist in the strong sense. Nevertheless, it may be; and that is why it can be included as a third example of a strongly reductionist account, in which religion and belief in God remain contexts of compensation, but on this account, the compensation is not in heaven, but here on earth.

A fourth example stays with childhood, in answering the question, 'Why believe in God?' with the answer, 'Because we have to'. This is the answer which says, 'Because I was born into it'. It is easy to overlook this example, because there are many who have been born into believing families and have subsequently rejected those beliefs, and some of the written accounts of that disentanglement have been memorable, to say the least – *Father and Son, The Way of All Flesh, Mark Rutherford*. Nevertheless, the fact of being born into a believing family is the context in which many people come to belief. When I was asking people (during the making of *Worlds of Faith*), 'Why are you a Hindu, Muslim, Christian, Jew, whatever?' almost invariably the answer came back, 'Because I was born like that.'[7] Certainly (as we have just seen), the consequence of belief is not inevitable, but it does create a strong constraint over subsequent outcomes in life, especially when it is translated into the assertion, 'Give me a child at 7 and I will make it mine forever.'

What is disturbing in that claim is its implication of compulsion, or of taking advantage of young people before they can make decisions for themselves. But that is not something that happens only to young people. Spiritual terrorisation occurs in all religions, and it constitutes a fifth example of strong compulsions in belief. William Sargent pioneered the exploration of this territory many years ago, in a book called *Battle for the Mind*. Although he subsequently modified the strength of his views, he nevertheless drew attention to the use of techniques akin to those of 'brainwashing', techniques of spiritual or psychological terrorisation, in order to induce a change of belief and behaviour in others, with vivid threats of hell-fire and the like. It is the interior equivalent of those external terrors against which Martin Gardner was protesting in the passage quoted earlier (p. 82). Phyllis McGinley reflected thus on 'The Theology of Jonathan Edwards':

> Whenever Mr Edwards spake
>   In Church about Damnation,
> The very benches used to quake
>   For awful agitation.
>
> Good men would pale and roll their eyes
>   While sinners rent their garments
> To hear him so anatomise
>   Hell's orgiastic torments,
>
> The blood, the flames, the agonies
>   In store for frail or flighty
> New Englanders who did not please
>   A whimsical Almighty . . .
>
> Abraham's God, the wrathful one,
>   Intolerant of error –
> Not God the Father or the Son
>   But God the Holy Terror.

It would be easy to go on adding further examples of strong necessity in the reasons why people believe; or if necessity is too strong, at least of powerful constraints which are controlling people into the outcome of believing in God. One of the most recent arrivals (to give a final and sixth example) is sociobiology – and this is by far the most aggressive in saying that you do not need God in order to explain why people believe in God. Sociobiology maintains (in more sophisticated form) the remark of Samuel Butler, that a chicken is an egg's way of making another egg. What sociobiology adds to Butler is that it says exactly the same of humans (well, not *exactly* the same, because humans do not have feathers); but what sociobiology claims is that we, as humans, are very complicated survival packages to enable the genes (the 'immortal genes') to replicate themselves. We are gene survival machines. What helps the genes to survive, in the human case, long enough to replicate themselves, is the fact that humans have also built defences outside the boundary of their skins. We have built houses, democracy, medical schools, and Dreadnought battleships. We have also built religions; and what sociobiology maintains is that since all enduring human behaviours have to be understood in terms of what they do (or what they have done in the past) to ensure or enhance the probability of gene replication, religions are decisively important examples of how this has been achieved culturally, because religions create and control societies in which family life and sex life are highly stable and highly ordered.

Thus sociobiology is an attempt to unify, on the one hand, the neo-Darwinian synthesis in understanding the process of evolution which has, among much else, produced the human species; and on the other hand, the consequences which that evolutionary process has produced in the human case – in other words, our individual, social and cultural behaviours. To put it in more precise language, sociobiology attempts to demonstrate the way in which the genotype programmes the conditions for its own continuity – that is, the replication of the genetic material and information. Sociobiology does not deny that the phenotypes (that is to say, the individual expressions of the genetic programmes) exhibit very varied behaviours. But the central point remains, that in the end all enduring behaviours, including those expressed in cultural forms, have (or have had) an adaptive value and significance: they help, in different ways, to protect the organism until its own genes are replicated (or at least until they can be). This means that all behaviours (including religious behaviours) and all beliefs (including beliefs in God) can be decoded as having a protective value and adaptive significance, in so far as they enhance the probability of gene replication. So the answer to the question, 'Why believe in God?' is, Because we are compelled to do so by the genetic programmes which evoke and lock on to those cultural experiments and explorations (including religion) which prove, in the long run, to be adaptive.

In fact, of course, the interaction between genes and culture is a great deal more complicated than that brief account makes it sound. To quote the summary of an anthropologist, Sol Katz:

> Biological evolution consists of a series of interactions among: the biological information resident within individuals and populations in the form of the genetic constitution (i.e., the DNA); the cultural information which is the sum of the knowledge and experience which a particular society has accumulated and is available for exchange among its members; and thirdly, a human central nervous system, which is of course a biologically based system, whose principal evolved function with respect to this model is to facilitate the communication or storage of individually and socially developed knowledge and awareness.[8]

This means that the future of the human species (supposing it has one) is contained in two separate information systems (the genetic and the cultural); and 'belief in God', on this account, is a result and an example of the one system protecting the other. It follows, further, that sociobiology can be strongly reductionist in relation to God, since 'God' is a symbolised source of control to ensure adaptive behaviours. Thus E. O. Wilson, the founding father of sociobiology, states specifically that *religions* will continue (because they are advantageous in evolutionary terms of enhancing the probability of survival), but that theology is finished: 'Theology is not likely to survive as an independent intellectual discipline. But religion itself will endure for a long time as a vital force in society.'[9]

God and the Supplementing of Reductionism

The fact that these six examples (of answering the question, 'Why believe in God?' with the reply, 'Because we have to') have been given briefly does not mean that they are being dismissed summarily. On the contrary, they clearly point to important truths in the data. But the fact also remains that believers can answer that question in exactly the same way. In other words they point to strong religious necessities – strong constraints which arise within the religious domain itself. Why believe in God? Because he died for my sins; because when I was still afar off he met me in his son and brought me home; because he revealed his will for me in the *sirat ulmustaqim* (the straight path which leads to heaven); because he guided our fathers through countless generations and laid his command upon us to be holy as he is holy.

All these are examples of religious necessities for those who see things that way. Clearly they do not evade the reductionist net, since people may be believing these things precisely because they are constrained to do so by social necessities, psychological necessities, family necessities. It is not the case that things become true simply because people can be found to believe them: they may be constrained into believing them for all or any of the reasons which we have already looked at. However, the point still remains that for those who do see events or people or signs or texts as revelatory of God, as the demand of God upon them, then that obviously does create a powerful religious necessity within them to believe in God.

What then happens for many (since the life of faith is not a calculus of propositions nor is it a matter of listening to lectures or, much, of reading books) is that the background propositions evoked from believing in God then receive their explication in the living of life with God and in the experience of living in that way. And that creates a further strong necessity – 'because I have to'.

Once again we are touching on a vast subject (the nature and interpretation of religious experience) by way of a brief allusion – and one that would certainly be in error if it gave the impression that there is one single experience which can be described as 'religious'. The term is a kind of shorthand for a very great complexity of consequences in human experience which occur in, and are derived from, specifically religious contexts, beliefs and practices. But as a shorthand, it does serve as a reminder that there are specific and distinct consequences which occur only in those contexts, and are not arrived at by any other route, despite all that has been claimed about LSD and hallucinogenic sacraments.[10]

What is certainly clear is that the experience of living

religiously (diverse though the explication of that adverb is) is an extremely powerful constraint. I remember asking one heroically admirable Christian, when I was making *Worlds of Faith*, whether she could understand or explain to me what she understood of the Trinity. She made a noble if faltering start, and then suddenly broke off and said, 'Look, do I really have to understand the Trinity before I pray to him?' The experience comes first, doctrine second. It was she also who went on to answer (when I asked her what the Sunday Eucharist means to her) in a way that is not derived from any manual of doctrine, but clearly makes every difference to her and to those whom she encounters and sustains:

I believe that I am receiving all that Jesus stood for. When Jesus was in the top room and he was having his last meal with the disciples, when they had the bread and they had the wine together, I think the whole meal represented his thirty-three years or so, and his few years of ministry, and I think it all came together in that room over that meal. And that's why I love our main meal in the evening, when we are all round the big table. It's a nice feel to it, and it's a very important meal to me in this family: I look forward to it, and we all get together: it's the togetherness with all the problems as well. Because Jesus had problems at the meal table: he had Judas whom he knew was going to betray him. And so it's very much really like our mealtimes, with all the friendship of the day, and anything perhaps that hasn't gone right for any of us – perhaps one of us is in a bit of a scratchy mood: it's all there at the table, you know. While we are having that meal, we are working through some nice family time together, and I think that's what Jesus and all the disciples were doing. Everything had come into the room that night; all the healing of the sick, all the rows that he had had with the Pharisees, all the teaching that he had tried to do with the disciples and perhaps they hadn't got it quite right. It was all there. And I think, finally, he just broke the bread up, you know, as we do our bread rolls – I think of that meal when we have, say, the crusty rolls, and we break them, because that's about the best way to do it. His breaking of the bread, I think, was his broken body, which was broken because of

92

all the suffering and the wrongdoing in the world: and I think that when I receive the symbol, I'm saying, 'Well, I hope that just by having this little bit, I can take away some of your pain; and by having a little sip of wine, that it will help to take away some of your pain'. And I think people are doing that right throughout the world. And perhaps, you know, for a bit, a lot of the pain does go; and that's perhaps what made it bearable for Jesus.[11]

It is obvious that this simple and yet immensely profound complex of experience (which can only occur in that way in its specific, religious context) is a powerful constraint over behaviour; and it clearly contributes much to the total network of constraint in producing, or sustaining, the outcome of belief in God. Furthermore it is one which does not have to wait for explanation before it can occur. Faith may seek understanding; but the transformation (or indeed the transfiguration) of life which may occur as a consequence of faith is often 'sufficient unto itself'. The experience comes first, the doctrine second.

Of course the interpretation of human experiences is never unequivocal. For one thing, it might still be possible to account for such experiences by means of strongly reductionist accounts. Equally experiences in religious contexts are not always confirmatory of beliefs: they may appear radically to contradict them. Thus the claimed experience of interaction with God includes 'the dark nights of the soul' – that much misused and so frequently misapplied phrase. Where it is appropriately used (that is, appropriate in relation to the appearances in consciousness which have evoked it), it points to experiences, for all their desolation, which lie *within* the relation to God, and not outside it. It is the experience which Martha O'Keefe, in her book *The Farthest Thunder*, believes that Emily Dickinson entered into, not as a matter of literary dependence (that is, not as a matter of reading St John of the Cross, because there is no evidence she ever did), but as a necessity within the progress of her own soul:

It was not Death, for I stood up,
And all the Dead lie down –
It was not Night, for all the Bells
Put out their Tongues, for Noon.

It was not Frost, for on my Flesh
I felt Siroccos – crawl
Nor Fire, for just my Marble feet
Could keep a Chancel cool –

And yet, it tasted, like them all,
The Figures I have seen
Set orderly, for Burial,
Reminded me, of mine –

As if my life were shaven,
And fitted to a frame,
And could not breathe without a key,
And 'twas like Midnight, some –

When everything that ticked – has stopped
And Space stares all around –
Or Grisly frosts – first Autumn morns,
Repeal the Beating Ground –

But, most, like Chaos, Stopless – cool –
Without a Chance, or Spar –
Or even a report of Land –
To justify – Despair.[12]

What, then, is happening within the experience which produces this and her other poetry? It is possible to interpret her, isolated in Amherst, as a neurotic recluse who was driven to write poetry as a substitute for the unrequited love in her life. And that may indeed be so. But what does she encounter which, as a consequence of its own nature, evokes the poetry about itself, and creates such differentiation in her reflection?

If the answer is 'nothing', then it is indeed very difficult to account for the immensely well-winnowed traditions of prayer and spirituality, in which the nearest resemblance or analogy lies in the encounter between humans which has evoked the language of love. It is that sense of *personal* encounter which had produced another powerful necessity in believing in God. So great has the urgency and involvement seemed to be that all religions have spoken of it in terms of sexual engagement and of the attraction which is loosely summarised as 'falling in love'. It is like love because it is physical and because it engages the whole of what we are; it is like love because, while it may be constant, it is not uniform (it has its ups and downs, its moments of intensity and of desolation); it is like love because it is not inevitable (it is as much a matter of grace as of graft); and perhaps even more to the point, it is like love because it is almost impossible to talk about – how can you talk about love, or describe it, when it covers such an immense range of very diverse phenomena? John Mortimer, in his play, *A Voyage Round My Father*, describes his father defending a wife in a divorce case, she having come under suspicion as a consequence of the attempts of her husband to observe her through binoculars from a tree:

> 'May it please you, my Lord, Members of the Jury. Love has driven men and women in the course of history to curious extremes. Love tempted Leander to plunge in and swim the raging Hellespont. It led Juliet to feign death and Ophelia madness. No doubt it complicated the serenity of the Garden of Eden and started the Trojan War: but surely there is no more curious example of the mysterious effects of this passion than the spectacle of Captain Waring of the Royal Engineers roosted in a tree complacently viewing the seduction of his beloved through a pair of strong racing binoculars.'[13]

Walter de la Mare made a very similar point:

> The commonplace summary 'he cannot really, then, have loved her' consists, for each one of us of five separate parcels each with its verbal label or tag . . . With how much of this will any other 'he' or 'she' be likely to concur in regard to those to whom the sentence might be actually applied? To Shelley and Harriet, or Swift and Vanessa, let us say: to Bothwell and Mary Stuart; George IV and Perdita; to Paolo and Francesca; Abelard and Heloise; to Thomas and Jane Carlyle; to Christian and his wife; Othello and Desdemona; to Gibbon and the young lady of whom (when on parental advice he had resigned her hand) he said, 'I sighed as a lover, I obeyed as a son' . . . Words indeed resemble chameleons, they take on the complexion of the minds that use them; and telepathy would scoff at them.[14]

What Walter de la Mare meant by telepathy is what would now be discussed under the heading of strict translation programmes and whether they are ever possible. But no matter how great the problems of translation to which, as a poet, he is referring, and no matter how great the ambiguities of cultural relativity are (which observe that what counts as love in one culture will not necessarily count as love in another), the fact remains that there is a sufficient possibility of intersubjective intelligence (despite the inevitable misunderstandings) for at least an approximate phenomenology of love to be constructed; and it is just as possible, despite the varieties of religious experience, to construct a comparable phenomenology of the consequences of God in meditation, prayer and contemplation.

We have already touched (pp. 72ff) on the foundations of phenomenology in relation to Husserl (though the practice of phenomenology has now moved a long way from his own programme). At the first level, phenomenology is concerned basically with recording and mapping reported data, without passing any value-judgments on the truth or virtue of what is being recorded – as a consequence of what, roughly, Husserl called *epoche*, bracketing-out presupposition. Thus one might undertake a first level phenomenological study on the attitudes of Americans to Russians without passing judgment on the validity, truth or value of the perceptions that are being reported. At the second level phenomenology attempts to get further and to ask: given the persistence and consistency of the reports that come in (where that is the case), what may we, and on occasion what must we, infer as a sufficient ground in reality to give rise to the reported appearances in consciousness, for them to occur as they do? Consequently phenomenology contributes to the question, 'Why believe in God?', on two different levels. First, it is simply mapping and reporting the varieties of what is claimed to be the case in the interactions between the human subject and what it takes to be God: thus it points to the consequences (sometimes very dramatic consequences in life and in experience) of attending to God in the ways that are appropriate (the point touched on already, pp. 77–80).

At this first level it is clear that the phenomenology of the experience of God (whether one wishes to offer strongly reductionist accounts of it or not) is extremely impressive, pointing as it does to a long-running and deep persistence in the data – that is, in the reports that come in of the consequences of attending to the possibility of God in the ways appropriate to it. Consequently at the second level phenomenology probes the issue of what we are entitled to infer as a sufficient ground in reality to account for the data by way of report, which it has been mapping at the first level: and in this enterprise, phenomenology is perfectly well aware of what we have already established, that our linguistic accounts of anything, including the universe, are always approximate, provisional, incomplete and corrigible. There is never any completely exhaustive account of anything, not even of something as superficially obvious as the universe, let alone of God. But, as we have seen, that does not in the least affect the fact that the accounts of God, as *mutatis mutandis* of the universe, are well-winnowed through time, because there is a deep persistence in the data in both cases. This is why theology is parasitic on the fundamental experiences which give rise to it by way of reflection.

It follows that experience (using that word as a shorthand, p. 91) is undoubtedly a strong constraint on belief. Nevertheless the fact remains that the interpretation of the data in the theistic case, not to mention the question of its validity, is by no means unequivocal. Therefore there remain searching arguments about the rationality of belief in God. Yet these too may provide another set of necessities, or at least of strong constraints, controlling some people into believing in God – into answering the question, 'Why believe in God?' with the answer, 'Because I have to.' The force of rational argument may seem a rather weak constraint, partly because we spend so much time not behaving rationally, and also because there are many who find the arguments *against* belief in God compellingly strong. That is true. But the fact remains that there are those who find the argument *for* belief in God comparably strong – and certainly strong enough to become a necessity for them. Indeed the same Martin Gardner whose heartfelt protest was quoted earlier (p. 82) wrote in the same book, *The Whys of a Philosophical Scrivener*, a record of how, almost (as he puts it) reluctantly, he came to conclusions which his friends would regard as unfashionable, to say the least: 'Why I am not an Ethical Relativist'; 'Why I am not an Atheist'; 'Prayer, why I do not think it foolish'; 'Immortality, why I am not resigned, why I do not think it strange, why I do not think it impossible' – to quote some of the chapter headings – including, 'Why I do not believe God's existence can be demonstrated'. But that is simply to make, in a different way, the point already emphasised, that reliability does not depend on absolute certainty. It may be, as Swinburne has argued extensively, that the arguments cannot point to more than probability, but if they do so, they cannot be regarded as negligible:

> I have urged that various occurrent phenomena are such that they are more to be expected, more probable if there is a God than if there is not. The existence of the universe, its conformity to order, the existence of animals and men, men having great opportunities for co-operation in acquiring knowledge and moulding the universe, the pattern of history and the existence of some evidence of miracles, and finally the occurrence of religious experiences, are all such as we have reason to expect if there is a God, and less reason to expect otherwise . . . On our total evidence theism is more probable than not . . . The experience of so many men in their moments of religious vision corroborates what nature and history shows to be quite likely – that there is a God who made and sustains man and the universe.[15]

So the fact remains – the fact as a matter of description, not of opinion – that the arguments are not foreclosed. As a matter of rationality God remains, at the very least (in terms of argument) what William James used to call, a live option.

James has in fact been much castigated for his version of pragmatism, because it has seemed to many to be saying that if a belief is pragmatically useful it thereby becomes true. Thus Russell in *A History of Western Philosophy*:

> With James's definition, it might happen that 'A exists' is true although in fact A does not exist. I have always found that the hypothesis of Santa Claus 'works satisfactorily' in the widest sense of the word; therefore 'Santa Claus exists' is true, although Santa Claus does not exist. James says (I repeat): 'If the hypothesis of God works satisfactorily in the widest sense of the word, it is true'. This simply omits

as unimportant the question whether God really is in his heaven.[16]

Perhaps it is for similar reasons that Cupitt derided traditional forms of belief in God as belief in a cosmic Father Christmas – with, equally, no reality.[17]

But although James often wrote and spoke in ways that invited criticism, and although under pressure he modified his pragmatism to take on board realistic considerations in relation to truth, nevertheless on this particular point he was not saying anything so unconsidered as Russell supposed; still less did it commit him to equating belief in God with belief in Father Christmas – as useful fictions which become true only in their usefulness. For James was perfectly well aware that live options can become dead options: is the earth stationary or moving round the sun? Is the earth flat or spherical? Once those were live options; now they are dead. At one early stage in life belief in Father Christmas's real existence is a live option; given the counteravailing evidence, it becomes dead. Making that decision *is* a matter of evidence, argument and interpretation – and that is why under pressure James conceded much more ground to realism than some of his earlier writings imply. What he certainly did maintain is that when an option *is* live, but there are insufficient grounds for deciding rationally, then there is nothing anti-rational, or irrational, in allowing our emotions (what James called our 'passional nature') to lead us.

But that is a very far cry from equating God with a cosmic Father Christmas, because the arguments for maintaining the independent reality of God are clearly sufficient, not to demonstrate God's existence, but to maintain the probability as a live option. That, at the very least, is a correct description of 'the state of play' – the ways in which the arguments are as a matter of fact still conducted, and their consequences by way of persuasion or insight for some people. So rational argument remains a strong constraint for some people in answering the question, 'Why do I believe?', with the response, 'Because I have to'.

How Do We Account for Human Behaviour?

All these have been examples of strong necessity or constraint in controlling people into believing in God. There are many other examples which could be added. But what does it leave us with at the end? Two lists of what appear to be contradictory, mutually exclusive sets of answers to the question, 'Why believe in God?' One set, the strongly reductionist, answers, 'Why indeed?' Belief in God is a human construction, a human invention; and when one thinks of all that has been done in the name of God, it would appear almost a blasphemy to believe. 'There is no social evil, no form of injustice, whether of the feudal or the capitalist order, which has not been sanctified in some way or another by religious sentiment and thereby rendered more impervious to change.' That was written, not by a paid-up member of the anti-God union, but by a Christian philosopher much concerned with the social implications of Christianity, Reinhold Niebuhr – he of whom William Temple once said, 'He is the troubler of my peace.'[18]

But then on the other side, there is the second set of answers which shows people connecting up with God in ways that set fire to life and burn out the frailty of our hypocrisy and fear and sin – a connection which then gets on with the translation of that experience and vision into life:

> Like anybody I would like to live a long life. Longevity has its place. But I am not concerned about that now. I just want to do God's will. And he's allowed me to go up to the mountain top. And I've looked over and I have *seen* the Promised Land. I may not get there with you. But I want you to know tonight that we as a people will get to the Promised Land. Well I'm happy tonight. I'm not worried about anything, I am not fearing any man, my eyes have seen the glory of the coming of the Lord.[19]

The words of Martin Luther King, not long before he was assassinated. Familiar words indeed; but in this case it is excessively unwise to let familiarity breed contempt. For belief in God has much to do with dreams, not just Freudian dreams, but with vision, with beholding the Promised Land and knowing that it will be reached even though, as Martin Luther King put it, 'I may not get there with you'. There is a power, there is a *dunamis*, as the New Testament called it, a dynamic, an effect, a transformation (and indeed the eventual transfiguration) of life which is a consequence of God.

So we seem to have two sets of contradictory answers, one dispensing with the reality of God, the other seeming to require it. How can we decide between them? The answer is that we cannot – or rather, much more to the point, we do not have to do so – nor should we try. Indeed to try to choose between them is to fall into the trap of the fallacy of the falsely dichotomous question – the fallacy which appears so often in exam papers and which bedevils discussions about belief in God. It is the fallacy which poses a question as though only one of two alternatives (to the exclusion of any other additional possibility) is correct and has to be chosen. The fallacy is to ask, for example, 'Concorde: white elephant or technological miracle?' The point is that it may be both those things – or neither – or indeed one but not the other – or much more besides.[20]

The point about these accounts (of why people believe in God) is that they may all be correct and may all be of effect in producing the outcomes of belief. It remains true that the *inferences* drawn about the reality or non-reality of God will be decided, if *all* such constraints are operating, because the inference drawn by those who operate a strongly-reductionist account (that the reality of God is not required to account for belief in God) will be contradicted if the inference from the second account (that the reality of God is required to account for the consequences of believing in God being of the idiosyncratic kind that they are) is correct. So the point here is crucial: all or many of the necessities or constraints described in those examples may in fact be operating at one and the same time; or to put it the other way round: it is *not* the case that we have to find (still less that we should be satisfied with) a single and comprehensive reason to account for belief in God – or for that matter, belief in anything. The reasons why things happen are always very complicated. If we wish to know why the Argentines invaded the Falklands, why stars collapse, why apples fall, why Caesar crossed the Rubicon, why people believe in God, it will be necessary to specify (at least theoretically) an immense network of constraints which have controlled the wave of possibility down into the outcome, into the eventuality of being what it is that is presenting itself evidentially or of behaving as it does.

It is true that the word 'constraint' sounds initially extremely negative; but constraints may in fact be very liberating: if you wish to play the piano, you have to accept the formal constraints of conventional notation, of time spent in practice, and so on; but by accepting the constraints, you may eventually be set free into the greater liberty of playing the piano or, indeed, of writing your own music beyond the constraints of conventional notation. If you wish to set foot on the moon (literally, in contrast to science fiction), it is only by understanding and accepting the constraints of gravity, atmosphere, relative motion, that you will be able, eventually, to build a rocket and do so. In the elliptical sentence (Ashby's) of cybernetics, 'Where a constraint exists, advantage can usually be taken of it.'[21]

The word 'constraint' overlaps, therefore, with such words as 'cause'. A constraint may be an active or immediate or proximate reason why something happens. Why did the glass break? Because I pushed it off the table. But the eventuality (the broken glass) was constrained into its outcome by much more than the immediate constraint (my pushing it) over its existing behaviour (resting on the table). It did not fly off to the moon, because it was constrained also by gravity. It was controlled into the outcome of breaking rather than remaining unbroken because of constraints derived from the different molecular structures of glass and (for example) iron.

Both active and passive, proximate and domain, constraints may therefore be specifiable in the *total* network of constraints which control a particular transformation of energy into its outcome – into its being the eventuality or occurrence which is making its demand on our attention, whether directly (for example, by observation) or indirectly (for example, by way of report of an event in the past).

In the case of human behaviour, the network of constraints controlling us into the outcomes in our lives (the things we do, or say, or imagine, or feel, or think) are immensely complex, and almost invariably beyond our powers to specify or describe. There are immediate constraints derived from the particular circumstance; there are constraints derived from our own perception and will; there are constraints over our behaviour derived from the genes and the genetic programmes; and at root, everything is constrained by the laws of motion. But if someone asks you, 'Why are you sitting in that chair?' and you say, 'Well, it's because of the attraction between masses which we refer to conventionally as gravity', that person is going to look at you very strangely. But that *is* a part of the network of constraint. The point is that we simply do not have the time to specify the whole network of constraint when we are trying to account for phenomena. So what happens, for the purposes of human enquiry (and this is why we have different school and university subjects), is that out of the *whole* network of constraints, we select or choose certain particular constraints and allow them to count for explanations. Thus in the case of an historical event, if we choose to specify only the social and economic constraints we may well end with a Marxist account; if we choose to specify only what has been going on inside the individual experience and perception, we may well end up with a psycho-analytic account; and so on. This also means (to look at it slightly differently) that we do not even have a single subject, 'history': we have social history, economic history, demographic history; and the reason why that is so is the same; out of the *total* network of constraints, some (of particular and singular importance, in producing particular outcomes) have been identified and isolated, we do not have to know everything in order to know something. Therefore in the way in which we saw earlier that reliability does not require absolute certainty, the same applies again: reliability does not require absolute completeness.

Nevertheless it is important to be clear that we are *not* giving complete accounts, but rather are making operational decisions about the kind of account we regard as sufficient. Consequently we are selecting the constraints which we believe to be relevant. They are *our* decisions about what is going to count as a sufficient specification of constraints, for whatever purposes of explanation we have set for ourselves. It follows that we cannot guarantee the superior validity of any one particular account of what occurs in the human case (except in relation to selected and specified goals) because any one account, like that of sociology, or that of economics, or of psychology, has simply abstracted from the *total* network of constraints one particular *set* of constraints. Certainly that set (the social, economic, psychoanalytic and so on) will have contributed to controlling an event into its outcome; but the fact remains that these are *choices* which we are making. They are choices about what we are going to count as sufficient by way of explanation, in relation to what we decide we are wanting to understand.

The catastrophe of strong reductionism is that, having identified perfectly proper, correct items within the total network of constraints, it then regards those items as the total and sufficient explanation; whereas what is necessary (however difficult it is to achieve) in the case of complex behaviour is a realistic generosity in the specification of constraints, if an adequate account of that behaviour is to be given. Take the example of schizophrenia: the term itself covers a spectrum of disorders, and no single or satisfactory explanation of what gives rise to them has been found (though theoretically it might be in terms of *proximate* constraint, as in the case of the virus which produces AIDS; but even then one needs a further specification of constraint to explain why some carriers of the virus express the consequences of the virus in actual illness and others do not). It therefore seems more likely that a network of constraints is involved than that a single constraint (for example, infant experience, genetic endowment, viral infection) has produced the outcome – as Bellak *et al.* (pp. 1f.) perceived long ago, though they put it in different language:

> So far, no convincing single explanation of the etiology or pathogenesis of schizophrenia has been produced. Bellak's attempt to find an answer has been formulated in the 'egopsychological multiple factor psychomatic theory of schizophrenia', wherein schizophrenia is seen as a syndrome caused by different etiological factors and pathogenic pathways, all of them sharing as final common manifest paths severe disorders of the ego functions.

Put more simply, we have to discern and specify an elaborate network of constraints which co-operate in producing the outcome known as schizophrenia. As Margulies (p. 255) put the point more recently: 'There is little real prospect of understanding processes which have genetic, behavioural, anatomical, electrophysiological, and biochemical attributes in the terms of any single discipline; useful descriptions of ordinary and pathological processes of brain might begin to consider the multiple dimensions of brain as a functional organ.'

So to take an example, suppose a straight line is constrained into the outcome of becoming a circle, and suppose there is a whole network of constraints which have controlled that straight line into the eventuality of turning up and round on itself, so that it becomes a circle: a strong reductionism simply isolates items within the set of constraints and says that (nothing but) *those* constraints are accounting for that phenemenon – that which presents itself evidentially.

Inverting the point, it now becomes clear that we cannot rule out a priori, the possibility that God, really and independently of ourselves, acts towards us and within us in such a way that his action must be included in the total network of constraints. So what is possible is that *all* the constraints, which were offered earlier in this chapter as examples, do belong to the delimitation of behaviour which we refer to as believing in God, but *without* the strongly reductionist conclusion. Yes, we do symbolise our strategies for survival; yes, we do promote God to preserve the status quo of privilege and exploitation in society; yes, we do project our unease on to a divine comforter; yes, we do express genetic programmes which incline us to postulate a protective figure. But yes, also, we do encounter a responsive and interactive Other when, for whatever constrained or abject motives in the first instance we reach out towards him from faith into love.

In this respect it is important to remember that the whole story of evolution is the story of constrained and increasingly complicated organisations of energy interacting with their available environments and eventually exploring and extending the range of what those environments might be: fish swim, animals walk, birds fly. It is the human organisation of energy which has carried this exploration furthest, out into space and indeed to the event-horizons of the universe: the whole universe is becoming the environment with which we are able to interact. What religious and theological history suggest is that the furthest (so to speak) event-horizon is the one discovered and explored in worship and in prayer. It sounds strange to speak of God in terms of an environment in which we live or as an event-horizon with which we can interact – though de Chardin was surely right to speak of *le milieu divin*. If the analogy were pressed to suggest that God is an alternative universe, clearly it would be absurd. But the fact remains that the extremely complex organisation of available energy which constitutes the human way of being does seem to be encountered by a reality which acts towards it in ways more like that of a person than of any other occurrence in our experience. This means that we can accept that all our motives for believing in God may be deeply constrained and formed by precisely those considerations which *in themselves* certainly do not require God to account for believing in God. But equally we cannot rule out, for that reason, the possibility that some constraints over what happens in the forming and transforming of our life are derived from God – or, more circumspectly, from what happens in the reality of the encounter with what we take to be God – the encounter which evokes the language about God, since *some* language is required to speak of what becomes common, recurrent and persistent in widely shared experience. We speak, not in order to say something final and complete, but because we must say something of that which lays unmistakable demand upon us. '*Aut tace aut loquere meliora silentio*';[22] and that alternative is difficult to do in the case of God.

If this seems complicated, there is at least some analogy in the way in which Freud was compelled to change his mind on what he originally thought about sex. In his original view, we approach the other in the case of sex with abject and neurotic motives, which Freud summarised (in part) as libido. We create that 'other' in the image of our own need and fantasy; and some remain locked into that diminished and impoverished understanding for ever. So on the one hand love, according to Freud, represents desire and frustration in the ego, as in this passage: 'Being in love is based on the simultaneous presence of directly sexual tendencies and of sexual tendencies that are inhibited in their aims, so that the object draws a part of the narcissistic ego-libido to itself. It is a condition in which there is only room for the ego and the object.' But there is in this case a responsive other, which, *by* its response, enables the transcendence of the need, the abject point of departure: 'Love in itself, in the form of longing and deprivation, lowers the self-regard; whereas to be loved, to have love returned, and to possess the beloved object, exalts it again.'

This means that there is, according to Freud, a sequence of instinctual libidinal energy seeking an object; of the object responding in effect; and of the consequent relationship wholly transcending the desire/frustration point of departure. The ontological reality of the other – the response of the other in the encounter (with all his or her neurotic need as well) – the otherness of the other in response – does create a limit on our fantasy, a disturbance like a rock in the midst of the river's flow. It is this which enables us, by the matter-of-factness of its own reality, to move far beyond the abject points of our departure. It is to be educated, as Freud used to put it, 'into reality'. Consequently Freud came to recognise and allow in his own system, not only the language of libido, but also the language of *liebe*, of love.

The same also clearly happens in the case of God: yes, no doubt we approach the possibility of God for all sorts of abject, wish-fulfillment and neurotic motives; and yes, for sure, we create God in the image of our need and fantasy – and some religious people remain locked into that impoverished understanding. But the apparent response of the Other, especially in the modes of interaction which are usually referred to as worship and prayer – the discovery of the Other creating consequence in the outcomes of our lives – has seemed to many to be a comparable disturbance, a comparable 'rock in the stream', which *is* its own reality; and as a result of that engagement, in this area as in the other, we are able to be moved far beyond what are undoubtedly the abject points of our departure. But that movement requires the reality and independence of God to set a limit on fantasy and to donate its own nature to ourselves: 'Blessed be God', as John Donne put it, 'that He is God only and divinely like Himself.'

So the real reason for believing in God is because, like Everest for Mallory, she is there; and because the attempt to climb that particular mountain produces its unmistakable consequences in behaviour. Above all, we cannot rule out the possibility that among the whole network of constraints which control our behaviours into being what they are, there are constraints derived, not by our own effort, but by grace, from an interactive reality correctly referred to as God.

This was a point I raised on a Radio 3 discussion with Ed Wilson (the founding father of sociobiology). I put the issue to him in this way:

> Manifestly, the genes and biological processes that you call the epigenetic rules are among the set of constraints, but I would want to argue that the set of constraints is very much wider than the genes and epigenetic rules. Indeed, you will know from of old that I would want to say that you cannot rule out the possibilty that constraints are being derived in the religious case from an interactive, responsive Other which has traditionally been referred to as God. So the word constraints seems to me to help your programme because it loosens it up at the seams; but, of course, it may be threatening to you, because it threatens the comprehensiveness of your theory.

Wilson replied:

> I think Bowker has stated a viewpoint which is very widespread among theologians and ethical philosophers that is hard to put into some kind of testable form, but which is certainly logical and valid. Among ethical philosophers, for example, a central question is whether or not ethical precepts exist outside of the human mind and the idiosyncracies of human evolution. In other words, the question is: Do our ethical precepts, what we believe to be right and wrong, merely represent products of our evolutionary history, or are we, through genetics and culture, tracking an external set of ethical precepts which we do not yet have the wit or the logical apparatus to recognise, but which somehow, blindly, we are moving towards. I believe that really is the central question of ethical philosophy.

At that point John Maddox, the chairman of the discussion, intervened to comment, 'To which you, I infer, have no answer yet.' Wilson replied:

I have none. As a scientific materialist, and now we are talking metaphysics and epistemology, as a scientific materialist I prefer to go my own materialistic route of assuming, as a working hypothesis, that we will eventually explain all of ethical behaviour and ethical precepts as the outcome of genetic evolutionary processes: but I certainly respect and am greatly bemused by the alternative explanation, I think alluded to by Bowker.[23]

'Bemused' no doubt: because that response is to fall into exactly that trap of the fallacy of the falsely dichotomous question (p. 101). As there, so here: it is not a case of *either* tracking an Absolute *or* expressing genetic programmes: it may be both/and. What the genes construct in the human case is necessarily genetically programmed; and those programmes undoubtedly induce it into explorations of a wide-ranging kind, and are surely rewarded in certain ways of life, which then get prescribed in transmissible rules. Nevertheless it may *also* be the case that, on the basis of those programmes, the organism in question makes genuine discoveries beyond itself, which are not directly constructed by the genetic programmes. We may indeed be programmed into being the sort of animal that makes the sorts of discoveries that we do.

Thus in the end we are driven back inevitably to the question of ontology – to the question of what we are entitled to infer in reality as a sufficient ground for the sorts of discovery that we make – as much in the case of the universe as in the case of God. In both cases (radically different though they are), there *is* a limit set upon our language by what exists independently of ourselves or of our approximate languages about it. Our languages will remain approximately wrong. But in the case of God, they are approximately wrong, I believe, about some One. It is true that here we see through a glass darkly, but at least we are beginning to see; here it is not yet made manifest what we shall be, but at least we are already fellow citizens with the saints and of the household of God; here we are still on the journey, but at least we are on the way.

So the power of religions may issue in the grim insanities of a systems-related behaviour. But it begins in the discovery of what this strange architecture of atoms and molecules is truly capable of being and of becoming for good, particularly when it accepts itself as a gift from God. It is because that sense of both the suffering and the sovereignty of God, in relation to the providence of his creation, is so profound (and so important for those who know it or know of it) that religion may be (and often is) the source of virtually everything that is good, yet equally it may be (and often is) the source of so much that is evil. Between the two stands our own vocation into God, and the issue of how seriously we accept it. For it is not religions, in the abstract, which are the agents of evil: it is people. Maybe if we trusted the experience of God as being the experience of *God* (with all the immensity which that implies), then, perhaps, we would be more careful, and certainly more critical, in protesting against those abuses of the necessity for systems which issue in insanity. Even more to the point, we might feel less urgency in ourselves to control the beliefs and behaviours of others into conformity, if we remember that to know something we do not have to know everything; and that God will always lie beyond a complete description while still inviting us to live in him for ever. *Deus semper maior:*

> And winds do go that way at noon
> To their ethereal homes,
> Whose bugles call the least of us
> To undepicted realms.

We began with that poem of Emily Dickinson. It is appropriate to make another poem of hers the end, the description of the setting out on that journey which any of us, "the least of us", can make. It speaks not of insanity, but of its near (though in fact unrelated) relative, of passion and of a consequence in love, which can be the enduring possession of us all:

> Exultation is the going
> Of an inland soul to sea –
> Past the Houses,
> Past the Headlands,
> Into deep Eternity –

Bred as we, among the mountains,
Can the sailor understand –
That divine intoxication
Of the first league out from land?[24]

Appendix

Religions as Systems*

The Mistrust of Systems

Why do we mistrust so much the institutions, the systems, the bureaucracies – the Juggernauts, as the title of a recent book described them[1] – which control our lives? Because we know only too well – only too frequently, not least in the last fifty years – what the highly organised system is capable of doing to individuals: the rise and fall of Hitler, the ruthlessness of Stalin, the catastrophe of Kampuchea, the continuing exploitation of one part of the world by another, and whatever else one can bring oneself, with a heavy heart, to add to the catalogue of organised and systematic evil: how is it possible to be alive at such a time and not be deeply protestant against the abuse and exploitation of power? Indeed the very term 'the system' has acquired overtones of an enemy to be opposed and defeated. 'Screwing the system' is the blunt phrase through which this protest has come to be expressed.

But it is not simply a case of 'them' against 'us'. Max Frisch, in his play *Andorra*, put all of us on trial, in what he called 'a model' of our responsibility in the destruction of Andri, who is, as the underlying Greek suggests, Everyman – as victim.

> *The Soldier, now in civilian clothes, enters the witness box.*
> SOLDIER I admit I never liked him, I didn't know that he wasn't a Jew, everybody said he was one. I didn't like him from the start. But I didn't kill him, I only did my duty. Orders are orders. What would the world come to if orders weren't carried out? I was a soldier.[2]

*First published in *Believing in the Church*, Report of the Doctrine Commission of the Church of England. SPCK 1981.

What would the world come to if orders were not carried out? The problem is that the world would not come to anything – indeed the world could not have come into being in the first place – if there were not a systematic, constrained and organised transmission of energy and information, an *ordered* process, organising available energy, against the tide of entropy, into regular and eventually self-replicating systems. It is that which creates the paradox and the tension between the individual and the system.

That may of course seem a rather different sense of 'orders' and 'control', but there are connections between the elementary and the complex organisations of energy which make it clear that no matter how much our sympathies may (and often must) be with the individual in relation to the system, organised systems are *necessary* for the continuity and transmission of information. That is as true of religious systems and religious information as it is of anything else (bearing in mind that both expressions are being used in a technical sense, and that the concept of information in this technical sense includes much more than verbal information). That is an important reason why there are religions, and why also, within Christianity, there are both the Church as the body of Christ and the churches as the sub-systems which help to constitute that body, enabling and continuing its life. And that too is why there *must* be 'corporate believing': it is necessary and inevitable in a universe of this sort.

Once we grasp this with sufficient understanding, then we are in a wiser position to be on our guard against the exploitation and abuse of this necessity. The institutional churches, as organised systems, are just as capable as any other systems of making, not a virtue but a vice out of a necessity – of being, as Geddes MacGregor once put it, 'a Scarlet Woman, Devil's Harlot, Satan's Whore' – on which he commented: 'The language is sixteenth-century in its robustness, the phenomenon is twentieth-century, at least equally and perhaps even *par excellence*.'[3] The purpose of this appendix is to give a brief indication of the ways in which religions can be understood as systems, processing and making available information which humans have regarded as being of fundamental importance – more important, potentially, than any other information, since it transmits from life to life, and from generation to generation, 'the Way, the Truth and the Life'.

Since this way of gaining insight into the nature and necessity of organised religions is not extensively known, and since also (unhappily) it is laden with technical terms, not all of which can be eradicated, it may be helpful to offer a brief indication of the ground to be covered:

1 *Systems and the organisation of life.* Human lives are now frequently understood as organised systems through which energy flows and is put to work in many different ways. One of the forms which energy takes in a universe of this sort is that of 'information': thus human beings are often now described as 'information-processing systems'. This is, at first sight, a strange sense of information, and an unfamiliar way of gaining insight into the complexity of human nature. So in this section a *brief* indication is given of why this approach is helpful and necessary.

2 *Systems and the process of information.* The process and transmission of information, in the human case, is *so* important that it has never been left to chance: it is channelled, protected and organised in ways which require systems for those purposes.

3 *Religions as systems.* Religious information is no exception to this, and thus organised religions appear as systems to protect information which is believed to be of vital (indeed saving) importance.

4 *Religions and boundaries.* The maintenance and continuity of a system demands some sense of a boundary – some way of marking what the system is, who belongs to it and who does not, who controls it and makes decisions within it, how the system is related to its environment (to whatever lies outside the boundary). Some examples are given of the problems this raises, and attention is drawn to the *limitations* of this method and style of analysis.

5 *The appropriation of resources in religious systems.* One limitation is that a systems analysis of religions cannot place sufficient emphasis on the fact that it is *individuals* within such systems who appropriate and internalise (make their own) the resources which religious systems mediate or make available. A fundamental reason *why* religions emerge as systems to protect 'saving knowledge' is precisely so that what is

offered in and through the systems can be taken up by individuals and can lead to the transformation/transfiguration of life, and thus to the ultimate goals of salvation (or the equivalent) which are pointed to in any religious system.

6 *The individual and the system.* But that leads to a potential (and often actual) conflict between the individual and the system. How can this conflict be handled? And how can it be made creative and liberating, rather than destructive and threatening?

Systems and the Organisation of Life

Let us suppose that you and I have never met before, and that we first encounter each other in the way of business or inquiry, as did Mr Pickwick and Samuel Weller over the top of a pair of boots, the personal property of a farmer who was refreshing himself with a slight lunch of two or three pounds of cold beef and a pot or two of porter after the fatigues of the borough market. Much may then ensue in the way of further acquaintance. But even at the first moment of encounter I already know a great deal about you. Indeed *superficially* I could claim to know almost everything about you. I know that you have one or two feet (or conceivably none), but certainly not four trotters like a pig; I know that you have one or two arms (or conceivably none), but not eight tentacles like an octopus. I know that you were conceived and born in much the same way as other human beings were conceived and born. I know that given sufficient time you will grow to a height between two feet and eight feet, and I know it is highly likely – though not absolutely certain – that one day you will die.

All this I know about you because our lives are set within very clear *boundaries* of possibility; and the codes of information, which run particularly through our genetic inheritance (through the genetic code), ensure that we will be constructed within these boundaries. I know, therefore, that you will have to construct a lifeway, so long as you remain alive, within those boundaries, in which you will attempt to hold your life together and bring it to whatever outcomes you believe or hope are possible, from day to day, and from

115

year to year. Obviously, there will be many problems and limitations, many things which threaten the continuity and success of your lifeway, not least death. But you have the intelligence to scan and understand what is going on around you, and you are able to plan and project a lifeway which will keep you in being; though for many people it is a mockery to talk of 'plans' and 'projects', when their lives are so close to bare subsistence or when they are crippled by a ravaging accident or disease.

Still, the basic fact remains that we are all consequences of the transmission of information through the genetic code, and that is why it is possible for me to know a great deal about you, even though we have never met. And yet, when I have listed all these items, like legs and chromosomes and arms and toes, you may well feel that I hardly know you at all. Such generalities hardly say anything about what you are as a person. And that is indeed a curious and important thing: you are a *person*, not a parcel of matter being posted from birth to death. So what is it that contributes this added dimension, of which I can know very little – indeed nothing – unless I meet you or read about you or hear someone talk about you?

It is of course the fact that you are informed by much more than the genetic code; or to put it the other way round, the genetic code constructs you in such a way that you are eventually capable of incorporating energy (transacting energy through your own body), not only in the form of breakfast but also in the form of signals which you are able to interpret as a fairly reliable indication of what is happening all around you – in your environment. The genes constructed you as a transaction of energy capable of processing information: the complicated accumulation of atoms and molecules inside your head, genetically coded into a non-random arrangement – the almost unbelievable complexity of chemistry and electricity which functions in that very tiny space – creates in you a consciousness of yourself and of your environment; a consciousness which because it has through time achieved a code of words, is able to interpret itself to itself, and is also able to share its interpretations, its hopes, its feelings, its understanding with other people. Therefore, in a way which we are far from fully understanding, you are

116

able to transcend the material analysis of what you are, in the way you live and move and have your being; in imagination you can go to the moon or fly with Peter Pan through the nursery window, when in fact your body is gravitationally anchored to the bed. From your genetic inheritance and from your interaction with your surroundings when you are born and as you grow, you become an informed subject.

The human organism, then, is constructed genotypically, like other living organisms, but phenotypically it is diversified; or to put it more simply we are all very similar in the general way in which the genes construct us, but we are very different as individual examples of human being. One source of diversity obviously occurs in the 'shuffling' of the chromosomes in sexual reproduction; but an equally important source of diversity is more *cultural* than *genetic*, and it lies in the capacity of a human being to become an informed subject. How does that happen? That question can be answered on two levels: the first is the investigation of how the brain functions as a receiver, storer and transmitter of information (remembering, as will be stressed again, that information in this technical sense is not confined to verbal communication); the second is the recognition of the many resources from which coded information-flow is derived in the human case – such things as parents, family, school, friends, television, newspapers, pop concerts – or in other words whatever can be specified in the environment in which a person actually lives and grows:

Now I am old and wait
Here in my country house in quiet Greece.
What have I gathered?

I have picked up wisdom lying
Disused about the world, available still,
Employable still, small odds and scraps of wisdom
A miscellaneous lot that yet makes up
A something that is genuine, with a body,
A shape, a character, more than half Platonic
(Greek, should I say?), and yet of practical use . . .

I have learned another lesson:
When life's half done you must give quality
To the other half, else you lose both, lose all.

Select, select: make an anthology
Of what's been given you by bold casual time.
Revise, omit: keep what's significant.
Fill, fill deserted time. Oh there's no comfort
In the wastes of empty time. Provide for age . . .
Set up the bleak worn day to show our sins,
Old and still ageing, like a flat squat herd
Crawling like sun on wall to the rim of time,
Up the long slope for ever.

Light and praise,
Love and atonement, harmony and peace,
Touch me, assail me; break and make my heart.[4]

In the anthology which is our life it is important to remember
that we also pick up cues of information directly from the
environment – directly from experience of the universe as we
interpret it through the patterns we have built up and through
the language we have acquired; and much of this information-
flow may be entirely without words. In discussing this in
The Religious Imagination I quoted a poem by Wordsworth to
illustrate this point, but it is not difficult to find other
examples. Here is a poem by Tennyson:

Tears, idle tears, I know not what they mean,
Tears from the depth of some divine despair
Rise in the heart, and gather to the eyes,
In looking on the happy Autumn-fields,
And thinking of the days that are no more.

Fresh as the first beam glittering on a sail,
That brings our friends up from the underworld,
Sad as the last which reddens over one
That sinks with all we love below the verge;
So sad, so fresh, the days that are no more.

Ah, sad and strange as in dark summer dawns
The earliest pipe of half-awaken'd birds
To dying ears, when unto dying eyes
The casement slowly grows a glimmering square;
So sad, so strange, the days that are no more.

Dear as remember'd kisses after death,
And sweet as those by hopeless fancy feign'd

On lips that are for others; deep as love,
Deep as first love, and wild with all regret;
O Death in Life, the days that are no more.[5]

In that poem by Tennyson, signs or cues of information arrive from his experience of the universe – the autumn fields, the ship's sail, the sunset – and those cues remind him of the deep and underlying consciousness of the passing of time, and of all that might have been and cannot now come to pass. The actual imputs are non-verbal, although of course they are immediately verbalised and interpreted in the existing brain state. As I summarised the point in *The Religious Imagination:*

> It must be emphasised that transmission does not necess-arily occur in verbal forms alone. Often, in the religious case, it is least of all in these. Consider the Bishop, in Chekhov's story of that name: his emotions are evoked in the opening pages through a whole succession of infor-mational inputs which do not occur in discernible words at all, although the background murmur of prayer is one of them. In some forms of Zen Buddhism much emphasis is given to 'transmission outside the Scriptures', in the silent relation between teacher and disciple; but it is not denied that transmission is taking place.[6]

Systems and the Process of Information

So non-verbal information flow should not be underestimated. Nevertheless words are clearly of supreme importance in the building up of the human mode of being, and in consequence human beings have not usually left the process of information entirely to chance. They have not allowed the transmission of information from one life to another, or from one generation to another, to be entirely accidental. Contexts of information process have been elaborated, or sometimes have simply developed, because of the inherent necessity for information process to be non-random. These elaborations or develop-ments may be gradual (as in the long development of an educational system) or they may be more sudden and

APPENDIX

deliberate (as in the introduction of a propaganda ministry in Germany in the 1930s).

What is certainly the case is that, whether devised or developed, means of information process can be of very considerable complexity. Schools and universities are an example of the way in which human beings have devised contexts in which information-flow and information process can occur, and in which children or adults can become 'informed consciousness' in particular areas of human knowledge and understanding. Religions equally are systems of information process. They are contexts in which information-flow, and in this case primarily religious information, is intended to occur. Each religion is a system – or more often a complex of sub-systems – in which fundamental resources of information are designated and are linked to a set of goals which lives may attain (usually lives informed from those resources). As Emerson observed, 'A man is a bundle of relations, a knot of roots, whose flower and fruitage is the world.' The goals may be near at hand or far-reaching, or, in other words, they may be proximate or ultimate. They may be proximate in the sense that more immediate goals may be held out as attainable – such goals as the forgiveness of a particular offence or sin, the securing of a better harvest, the death of your malignant neighbour's cow, an act of love and charity towards your neighbour; or they may also be ultimate, in the sense that salvation, *moksha*, nirvana and the Elysian fields are held out as attainable – as also are such goals as Gehenna, the *pretaloka* and the cheerless fields of Asphodel.

The basic point which underlies all this is simple and important: *information (whether verbal or non-verbal) does not slop around in the universe in a random or arbitrary manner.* It is channelled and protected, coded and organised; and precisely for that reason the construction of complex organisms and highly complicated behaviour is possible. At the social and cultural level, information is not left to chance either. It is not simply religions which have to be systematically organised in order to protect and transmit (make available) fundamentally important opportunity and information, which, in so far as it is incorporated or internalised in any individual life, changes the character of that life or changes what happens in the

120

actual living of that life.[7] Trade unions, political parties, professional football, Marks and Spencer's, the Royal Air Force, British Leyland, the United Nations, as well as the Church of England (or a province or a diocese or a deanery or a parish) have to be *systematically* ordered if continuity is to be assured (or at least attempted), and if decisions affecting the organisation are to be made and implemented; and there are effective and ineffective ways of achieving this.

We can see a comparable process at work in the case of the natural sciences. The information which constitutes the understanding of the universe (and the means to that understanding) which we refer to as 'natural science' is not shared and transmitted in a wholly random or haphazard manner (no matter what it occasionally feels like in a particular classroom). Nor can we possibly understand 'the whole of the universe' in a single act of comprehension (except in the non-science holistic experience of a mystic). The sciences are necessarily broken down into sub-systems of technique and understanding; and the community of (say) physicists has its own systematic control systems and systems of value and approval. Books like that of Daniel Kelves (*The Physicists: The History of a Scientific Community in Modern America*)[8] or of Horace Judson (*The Eighth Day of Creation: Makers of the Revolution in Biology*)[9] make the organisation of the control and transmission of scientific information abundantly clear. As Barnes summarised the point, with reference to scientific education, 'transmission of the current paradigm is the key point': 'Science is not a special kind of knowledge source; it has to face the problem of credibility, and the technical constraints facing the transmission of culture in any context.'[10]

Religions as Systems

Religions too have to face the problems of credibility and transmission. Different religions (or to be more precise the authorities or operators of a particular system) solve the problems in different ways: some draw clear and strong boundaries in order to designate who is in and who is outside the system, what counts as orthodox believing, and what counts as appropriate or inappropriate behaviour, with a strong hierarchy of decision and control (examples are Roman Catholicism and Sunni Islam); others draw loose boundaries and are less concerned with the clear determination of who is in and who is outside, or with the specification of orthodoxy and unorthodoxy (examples are Anglicanism and Mahayana Buddhism; though note that in both cases there may be extremely strong *sub*-systems – highly organised and hierarchical – within the more general system; and note also that the general system designates *some* boundary markers).

But even in religious systems which are less boundary-minded or boundary-concerned, the fact remains that in Christianity as (*mutatis mutandis*) in any religious system, resources are offered and are made available (word and sacrament, community, inspiration and judgment) which do not 'slop around in the universe', but which are channelled and protected (particularly in ritual); and goals are offered, both to those within the system/church and to those outside, which are both proximate (changing life by love) and ultimate (the realisation of our redemption and the vision of God). This immediately illuminates why adherents to religions are so passionate – not only in the ways that can be illustrated from the contemporary political scene, but also in the long history of religions which made Winwood Reade include them very firmly in the Martyrdom of Man. They are passionate because many of the goals held out in religions as attainable are indeed of ultimate importance: they have to do, not only with life, but eventually with the possibility of life beyond life.

This also makes it very clear why religions as systems of information process necessarily produce mechanisms of transmission and control. It is necessary for there to be both a connection between the fundamental resources and the lives that have to be lived, and also some means of monitoring the appropriation of the resources into life, and the appropriateness or otherwise in terms of outcome. The resources may be strongly defined in terms of content (as in the case of Scripture, the Torah, the Quran or Sruti) or loosely defined (as in the case of a guru, the words of an oracle, the Holy Spirit). At the furthest extreme there may be 'transmission outside the Scriptures', to quote again the Buddhist phrase, and there may be transmission by association, without any observable communication taking place: but transmission is still, by definition, claimed to be occurring.

Monitoring what is going on – that is, trying to ensure, both the process of information flow into other lives and other generations, and also the appropriateness of the actual outcomes when matched against what the resources themselves designate as appropriate, is served by an enormous range of different means, depending very much on the geographical extent of the system in question. It is much easier to ensure transmission and appropriateness in an African or an Indian village than it is to ensure it in the Roman Catholic Church. Yet what we know for certain is that, in the history of religions, what we are always observing are repeated attempts to enhance the formality (and effectiveness) of the system. We may be observing much else beside that, but *that* we are certainly always observing, just as we are always observing its counterpart, the protest against it – and to that highly important protest we shall return. But before doing so, we may ask: How can such a diffuse reality as Christianity be systematised? In other words how can it function as a system in this formal sense? The answer is that *it* cannot do so. Christianity may be defined as *Quod semper, quod ubique, quod ab omnibus creditum est,* but in fact from the same resource (Scripture and tradition) have been derived innumerable sub-systems; and the same is true, *mutatis mutandis,* of Judaism, Islam, Hinduism, Buddhism, Shinto and any other complex religious system.

There are two points to notice here: first the phrase, 'derived from the same resource': but it is characteristic of sub-systems that they add other legitimating resources. They may add the interpretation or teaching of a founding figure or of a contemporary teacher; and that teaching may supplement or even displace the basic resources of the system; thus the Moonies claim to be Christian in the American courts, by associating the teachings of Mr Moon with Christian Scripture.[11] Or again, they may add tradition as a supplementary and authoritative interpretation of the fundamental resource; and that may be done formally, as when in the Roman Catholic Church a dogma is defined which finds at best only tenuous justification in Scripture – like the Assumption or the Immaculate Conception; or it may be an informal association, as in the Muslim association of *hadith* with Quran, in which Quran remains absolutely distinct and more fundamentally authoritative. Or yet again, they may add the inspired utterance of an ecstatic or charismatic figure or of an oracle. In other words, although the designation of fundamental resources is characteristic of religious systems, in the sub-systems the connection with those resources may be very loose, or indeed non-existent; but connection with *some* designated resource remains basic.

The second point is this: it is also characteristic of sub-systems that some of them will claim nevertheless to be the whole system – or at least to be the authentic representation of what is meant to be the case. Sunni Muslims believe themselves to be the authentic continuity of Islam derived from Muhammad and the Quran; but so also do those many sub-systems referred to collectively as Shiites; and what is clearly at issue there is the *means* of continuity: *does* it have to be through the family of Muhammad and his descendants as Imams? Or again, Roman Catholicism has claimed to represent the authentic continuity from Christ and his apostles. With that claim has gone the construction of a strongly bounded system, with effective means of transmission and control: clear hierarchies of authority; the inquisition and the index; a heavy investment in education; the priesthood as father, and the confessional; the strong definition of the intermediate goals of behaviour; a common central ritual with (until recently) a common language of Latin.

Religions and Boundaries

So potentially religious systems or sub-systems are strongly bounded open systems. The concept of 'boundary' does not in the least mean that such systems are literally isolated. The concept of 'boundary' is a means of analysing action within a system, and interaction with its environment. To give a simple example, let us, *à la* Mrs Beeton, take one egg. A bird's egg is a bounded self-contained system whose 'action' is to support life for the developing embryo. All the necessary energy sources, the nutrients, minerals and water, are present in the new-laid egg; the parent bird or birds have nothing further to contribute beyond keeping the egg warm and occasionally turning it over so that the embryo does not adhere to the shell membranes. Yet even so, the strongly bounded system of an egg lacks one essential requirement, the fuel to drive the metabolism of the embryonic cells, and that fuel is oxygen. Oxygen has to be taken in through the boundary (through pores in the shell, first demonstrated by John Davy in 1863) from the atmosphere, and carbon dioxide has to be discharged. In fact it has been calculated that 'over the 21 days of its incubation a typical chicken egg weighing 60 grams will take up about 6 litres of oxygen and give off 4.5 litres of carbon dioxide and 11 litres of water vapour'[12] Even then the interaction across the boundary will not be sufficient to meet the goals of the system (the hatching of the chick), and on about day nineteen the chick penetrates the air cell at the blunt end of the egg and begins to ventilate its lungs; about six hours later it uses its increased energy to make a small hole through the actual boundary, the shell.

In that example the concept of 'boundary' clarifies the analysis of both the internal process of the system and the interactions with its environment. This means that the concept of 'boundary' is usually an operational definition in systems theory – an important definition, since, as H. R. Bobbitt *et al.* argue, 'without a boundary we do not have a system, and the boundary or boundaries determine where systems and sub-systems start and stop'. They then suggest:

> A *boundary* of a system is a closed line placed around certain objects so that there is less intensity of interaction *across* the line or among objects *outside* the line than among objects *within* the closed line. *Less intensity* means an intensity below some level, this level being a function of the problem under consideration. For example, we might consider communication, influence or work flow as the interaction variables.[13]

That means that *different boundaries can be drawn with the same organisation*, depending on which interaction one is studying. It follows that the defining of a system or of a sub-system is to a great extent a matter of opinion and decision on the part of the systems analyst; and in his analysis he must always be on his guard against reifying (turning into real objects) the interactions or the organisations which he is studying. What he isolates as a system or sub-system depends on what interactions, or what flow of information or of decision-making (or whatever) he wishes to understand more clearly. (It also follows that no single model of interpretation will ever be adequate.) Thus if one wishes to analyse the hierarchical flow of authority in a system, one will detach and schematise the authority figures and draw the boundary around the functioning of authority in the system. But if one wishes to analyse the process of research and development in a company, or the process of maintaining machines and buildings, then different boundaries will be drawn. But what is common to all of them is that they specify not only particular functions within the organisation, but also the interactions and interrelationships which obtain across the boundaries. Thus if a whole company is understood as a system the boundary of the company relates what goes on inside the organisation to what goes on outside it – its relation, for example, to its customers, its competitors, its shareholders, its suppliers, the Inland Revenue, and so on.

Such analyses can very easily be applied to religious systems and can help us to understand why and how religions continue themselves through time as they do. What sometimes emphasises the concept of boundary maintenance in the religious case is the fact that in some religious systems there is a concern with literal, geographical boundaries – with their own parish or territory. Until recently, for example, an orthodox Indian was not supposed to travel out of India or even out of his province; as Walker puts it, 'The brahmins of Panchala could not visit Vanga and those of Chedi could not journey to the land of Vidarbha. If they did so they were regarded as unclean until they had undergone the *prayaschitta* ceremony of purification.'[14] Or again, a hermit in his cave, or Simeon Stylites on his pillar, or a Dead Sea community in geographical separation, all exemplify an attempt at literal boundary maintenance.

Yet even they interact with their environment: even Simeon Stylites let down an occasional basket for food; and in that sense of interaction, such systems are open to systems analysis. It scarcely needs to be said how directly applicable this is to Paul, and to his understanding of Christianity as a system on the analogy of the body, with one obvious operational boundary being drawn around the hierarchy of God, Christ, man, woman in 1 Corinthians 11:3. The practical necessities of church organisation and management, traceable through the pastoral epistles and into the period of the Apostolic Fathers, led to the emergence of bishops, presbyters and deacons as the contingent hierarchy.[15]

It follows that the study of any complex system introduces *a necessary artificiality* if anything is to be learned about the behaviour of the system – what one might call a self-imposed limitation. To give an example: it is possible to study the energy flow through an individual organism, treating the organism as a thermodynamic unit, and observing the conservation and degradation of energy. In that case, the activities of its components, such as cells, can be ignored in detail. Exactly the same study of energy flow can be made – or attempted – for a whole ecosystem, because an ecosystem can be regarded as an 'individual'. In that case the activities of its components, for example species populations, can be ignored in detail. That is already one level of restriction. But the complexity of the ecosystem introduces further artificiality. As Phillipson put it: 'Generally speaking, studies of energy flow through ecosystems do take into account the different trophic levels: but this approach, although a simplification, has the disadvantage that many animals are omnivorous and cannot be assigned to any one level.' He therefore commented: 'The enormous task of studying energy flow both through, and within, a complex ecosystem restricts the research worker to an investigation of trophic levels as the components of the system, and the limitations of this approach will affect the overall study.'[16]

The complexity of systems means that we cannot understand the whole of a complexity in one large, single gulp of comprehension, like a Gollum attempting to swallow a Hobbit. The universe is intelligible only because it is highly redundant and reducible, not because we have to understand 'all or nothing'. Similarly religions are highly complex systems which cannot be understood as a whole. Provided that we are not alarmed by the kind of restriction which is introduced into the study of any systems, then we can certainly gain understanding of the behaviour of religious systems, and of why they behave as they do, without claiming that we are thereby understanding 'the whole of everything' about religions.

So the behaviour of a *system*, as opposed to the behaviour of participants *in* a system, is to be discerned in its functions, in its maintenance of its structure, in the efficacy with which it transforms inputs into outputs, and in its ability to identify novel stimuli, both internally and externally derived, and to take action which is appropriate in relation to the goals of the system – remembering that 'goals' are elusive: what are designated as goals in the system (in its theoretical construction mediated through such artefacts as teaching or texts) *may* scarcely coincide at all with an individual's proximate or ultimate goals (and in the Christian case there is an inherent contradiction in any case in talking of goals: the Christian's engagement with God and with his neighbour cannot be undertaken in order to reach 'goals'); nevertheless, descriptively, there are 'goals' or ends, such as the love and worship of God, which can be discerned.

But that immediately means that a system which endeavours to change the nature of itself *in via* – which attempts, as Neurath put it, to repair the boat while still at sea – is going to come under great strain. We see this (or used to see this) commonly when unions hear that an operations research team or business efficiency expert has just come through the factory gates; but we see it also, to go back to an earlier example, in Roman Catholicism at the present time. I gave examples of the highly efficient system which was developed in the process of Roman Catholicism through time. But many features of the system are being dismantled: the virtual disappearance of the Latin mass, the collegiality of bishops in relation to the pope at the Vatican (at least theoretically; not evidently in practice with the present pope, appearances notwithstanding), the erosion of sacramental and individual confession, the removal of the altar from the east end to the centre of the church, are simple and random examples of what is happening.

Such things may be highly desirable – and may be designated as desirable by reference to the legitimising resources of the system in question (in other words, by appeal to Scripture and tradition), but that does not alter the extreme disturbance caused to those, who, like the present pope, realise (even if only intuitively) that the transmission of information does not occur randomly in the universe but mainly through systematic means. What is at issue is not a particular piece of teaching or a particular example of bureaucracy, but the continuity and maintenance of the system as a whole. It is very difficult for those formed in and through one system, and for whom that system is still resourceful in their own case, to imagine what could conceivably take its place and have the same effect in transmission and control. So when we observe that the pope's advice in *Humanae Vitae*, subsequently reinforced by the Synod of Bishops in Rome, says one thing, and that the birth statistics of Roman Catholic parents say another, the consequences for the system and for the bonding of individuals to it far outweigh in importance the actual arguments about that particular issue.

However, the picture is not wholly gloomy. It is not a necessary condition of religious continuity that it should be boundary-minded in a strong sense. Anglicanism has notoriously infuriated Roman Catholics by its apparent unwillingness to draw its operational boundaries (for example, its means of determining doctrine) with formal and exclusive precision, though in fact there are very strong sub-systems within Anglicanism. Great virtues have accrued to Anglicanism by way of toleration and great virtues to Roman Catholicism by way of the disciplined and systematic pursuit of sanctity. But there is a price to be paid for each virtue.

What poses a great dilemma for *all* religious systems is that the human animal is increasingly becoming multiply resourceful – that is, drawing on *many* sources for its life. It may be the case that in an African or South American village there is still a single and integrated system. But even in such villages the transistor radio is frequently planted as carefully as the corn or the maize. Men and women are deriving information from a wide range of resources, some of them highly inimical to religious claims. There is nothing new in the multiplicity of resources. To give just one example, Lévi-Strauss coined the term *bricolage* to draw attention to this multiple resourcefulness at the most elementary level of myth-making: Lévi-Strauss derived the term from the verb *bricoler*, which referred originally to a movement out of the ordinary – to a horse swerving to avoid an obstacle, or to a ball rebounding or to the ricochet of a bullet. *Jouer la bricole* means to play off the cushion in billiards. So a *bricoleur* is a 'jack-of-all-trades', someone who improvises and uses whatever comes to hand, rather than employing purpose-built parts. *Bricolage* in myth-making and myth-using refers to the fact that the components have been used before and will be used again, and also to the fact that the myth-maker draws on whatever happens to be lying around that will suit his purpose. So human beings, or at least some of them, have always been openminded. But what *is* new is the extremely wide practice and acceptance of multiple resourcefulness, combined often with an emphasis on the restrictive and incapacitating consequences of being bound to a single system.

To some extent, this is a consequence of the revolution in communications and in the expansion of information. We are saturated by possibility – and there is a price to be paid for that as well. The world has become a bit like the famous Fred Hoey broadcast, which began with a kind of semi-Spoonerism, 'Good afternoon, Fred Hoey, this is everybody speaking.' There are very real problems for religious systems as a consequence of this revolution, and ones which demand extremely clearheaded analysis of their implications for the continuity of transmission within such systems.

But for the moment at least the systems remain in being – and in the case of at least one, Islam, we can see a religious system going through a process of re-enhancing its formality, by the reapplication of Islamic law in Iran and Pakistan. In others, for example Christianity, it seems likely that there will be continuing and (in some parts of the world increasing) diversity of interpretations derived from the same resource (Scripture and – with differing degrees of authority – tradition), believing themselves to be legitimate in relation to that resource; and it is predictable that these will develop their own means of continuity. The critical question will be how to establish a positive interrelationship of communication and trust between the parts (and this, from a systems point of view, is already a clear issue in covenanting), if it is to be held that they are sub-systems of the same system (Christianity) and are not new independent systems (new religions or sects). To take the example of a different system, the human family: various parts of the system (uncles, aunts, grandparents, children as they grow up) will pursue their own lifeways with considerable diversity yet still remain part of the same family. If the family is geographically restricted (living in the same area or even house) the expression of its life is more likely to be interactive; if it is dispersed, less so. But in either case issues may arise which create disturbance in the system. Some may be 'family rows' which affect attitudes and behaviour but which do not disintegrate the system. But others may seem, to at least some of the participants (family members), to be so disruptive that the system cannot contain the expression of them. 'Go, and do not darken my door again' may seem melodramatic but it has occurred (and still does) when certain behaviour contradicts fundamental beliefs, practices or values which have previously obtained.

In religious systems there may be similar 'family rows', issues which affect attitudes and behaviour but which do not disintegrate the system. There is considerable disruption in the sub-system of Christianity at the present time about grants made by the World Council of Churches to guerrilla organisations, but the dispute is not likely to create systematic schism. On the other hand, there are *other* issues where the disagreement is more profound – where, that is, a particular proposal seems to others to be so mismatched when judged against the fundamental legitimising resources that it cannot be contained in the system. For example, where it is proposed in a sub-system of Christianity that women should be ordained, others within that sub-system and in other sub-systems believe that that proposal cannot be matched and thus legitimised in the fundamental resource (Scripture and tradition). So serious does this kind of mismatch seem that it creates systematic separation, a breakaway church in the United States and a warning from Roman Catholics and Orthodox Christians that such a move will set back or prevent explorations towards reunion.

This, then, is a classic problem of boundary analysis, of analysing the necessary (or what are believed to be the necessary) conditions of continuity, and of the kind of interaction which obtains or fails to obtain within what formally appears to be a whole system; and it is this kind of analysis which is required if an ecumenical ambition is ever to be realised, both within a system, such as Christianity, and between systems, such as religions. But whatever the future may hold, it is in such systems – or rather in the sub-systems which constitute such systems – that human beings become (if we can use these odd phrases) Hinduistically informed or Islamically informed or Christianly informed – bearing in mind that those adverbs are broken up into many different forms of expression, and bearing in mind also the belief in all religions that their words, symbols, people, institutions, buildings and so on may be agents in the transmission of inputs derived from resources external to the system, such resources as God, or Brahma, or the Holy Spirit. But the general point is that from and within these systems there can occur an internalisation of available resources which then acts, or can act, as a constraint in the continuing construction of life.

The Appropriation of Resources in Religious Systems

For the participant in a religious system, what is offered as resourceful in the system is internalised, at least in part, and is expressed in the outcome of life – or should be, if the participant is not to be hypocritical in his or her allegiance: ' "A what, my good sir?" demanded Mr Pecksniff', when Mr Anthony Chuzzlewit told him bluntly not to be a hypocrite. ' "A what, my good sir?" . . . "A hypocrite." "Charity, my dear," said Mr Pecksniff. "When I take my chamber candlestick tonight, remind me to be more than usually particular in praying for Mr Anthony Chuzzlewit, who has done me an injustice." ' The real harm in hypocrisy lies neither in the prayer nor in the candlestick. If we all waited to pray until we were free of fault, the word 'prayer' would cease to exist in any human language. The real harm lies in the distinction in the *nature* of hypocrisy which Chuzzlewit made later on, when he encountered Pecksniff in the stagecoach, and when Pecksniff protested that while he may be a hypocrite, he is certainly not a brute:

'Pooh, pooh!' said the old man. 'What signifies that word, Pecksniff? Hypocrite! Why, we are all hypocrites. We were all hypocrites t'other day . . . The only difference between you and the rest was – shall I tell you the difference between you and the rest now, Pecksniff?' 'If you please, my good sir; if you please.' 'Why, the annoying quality in *you* is,' said the old man, 'that you never have a confederate or partner in your juggling; you would deceive everybody, even those who practise the same art; and have a way with you, as if you – he, he, he! – as if you really believed yourself.'

The distinction here is a critical one, because it emphasises the obvious, that the human appropriation and expression of religious resources or inputs is nothing like so simple or mechanical as the input, storage, retrieval and output system of a constructed information system, such as a computer. It is perfectly accurate, and with reference to many social and psychological issues extremely helpful, to regard the human form of energy transaction as an information-processing system. But the complexity, speed, efficiency and 'regular irregularity' (effective rule-breaking) with which that is done in the human case creates the awkward reality of diverse character – awkward, that is, from the point of view of the system or design theorist, not from the viewpoint of the artist, the poet or the person who has to live.

Heroic attempts are made in the design of organisations to eliminate what are known technically (or jargonistically) as 'unanticipated mean behavioural patterns': as early as the work of Taylor and Fayol – the inventor of Fayol's bridge, which designates levels of cross-reference in hierarchies – attempts were made to determine what an average man could and could not do, and to judge what he would and would not do, and then to build into the control system in the organisation, mechanisms which would constrain actual workers to work at the optimum level. But obviously the estimates of mean capacity were not an exhaustive set. It is the other variables which constitute the unanticipated mean sources of emergent behaviour. The analysis of these, although it has advanced greatly in sophistication since the time of Taylor and Fayol, remains necessarily incomplete, partly because of the huge range of variables, and partly because such analysis becomes a part of the set of possible behaviours and thus demands inclusion in the set of those possible sets; and since we can never arrive at the set of *all* possible sets, the analysis remains fruitful but incomplete. In practice, *what* is designed works back on those for whom it was designed, modifying their behaviour in unpredictable ways as they react to the design or programme.

But however much we rejoice that the human rat escapes from the experimental maze and dances its idiosyncratic pirouette on the grey hairs of the management design team, we must not lose sight of the equally fundamental truths that systems behave systematically; that religions are no exception to this, and that when we try to understand this we are in a much better position to demand or to ensure that they function more effectively and less oppressively. But the point of stressing diverse character and the idiosyncrasy of human behaviour is to raise the question, what is the *purpose* of a religious system? For this question brings us back on to characteristically religious ground. What is the purpose or the goal? Obviously not to increase exports or to improve profits – though occasionally the drive in a particular parish to pay for the new church hall, or to pay for the church schools, seems almost to have become the goal of a parochial system. But that is a proximate, or intermediate, goal. What is the overarching purpose, or ultimate goal, of a religious system? Certainly not to build bigger and better systems, though it is familiar in every religious system that some people *do* always emerge for whom the system is an end in itself: they become commissars, or they become inquisitors, or indeed some of them become university professors. But none of that is the purpose; it is the product of the systematic nature of systems. What is the purpose?

The purpose of the Christian system, and of the sub-systems which constitute Christianity, is to enable individuals to love God and to love their neighbour as themselves. The purpose of the system is to enable the worship and the adoration of God, in himself and in the service and stewardship of his creation. The purpose of the system is to make real among us forgiveness, redemption and atonement. The purpose of the system is to be the sign and way of salvation. It is to create a community in which men and women – together and alone – can be confronted by God and drawn into a union with him of love and praise.

It follows that what Christianity offers and mediates into human life is not created simply or solely within the system. Some of the particular resources which are, so to speak, on offer, *are* generated within the system. But some of the institutions and protected channels of communication in Christianity (for example, prayer and the sacraments) are believed to mediate a direct input or constraint into life which is derived from outside the system – which is derived, in other words, from God. It is precisely for this reason that in general Christianity has refused to be casual about the sacraments, and has, for example, 'protected' the special character of the Eucharist and the consecration of the elements, in its restriction of who may be the president or celebrant, in its caution about appropriate liturgy, and in its care to ensure that any remaining consecrated elements shall not carelessly be discarded ('shall not be carried out of the church', as the Prayer Book puts it, but shall be reverently consumed). The sacrament is a 'protected channel' of communication, in which the initiative comes from outside the system, and is then mediated through it. Ritual and sacrament are indispensable for the Christian system (in other words, for Christian life), given that this is the sort of universe in which we live, and which we believe is itself derived from God as 'the unproduced producer of all that is'.

So the first purpose of the Christian system is to draw us into the worship and adoration of God. But that implies a second purpose – to draw *us* into that vision; for it is also a goal in a religious system that we or any other human subject can be informed, can receive into the construction of a lifeway, those constraints of information which if they are appropriated and realised in life, can lead that lifeway to what the system in question counts as an ultimately successful outcome – to salvation, to the worship and love of God, and to the service and care of his creation.

The Individual and the System

It is true that human systems have a history and a life of their own, which is independent of the particular individuals which constitute them, even though *some* individuals *must* constitute them. Thus there is a history of parliament, a history of nursing, a history of higher education, a history of synodical government, which is more than the stories of the people who participate in these activities. Yet the fact also remains that an important locus for the process and trans-action of religious information and resources *is* the individual. And this creates precisely that tension and paradox with which this appendix begins: on the one hand, religious systems have to be organised if they are to mediate what they believe to be the words of life, or of salvation, or of truth, to individual lives; yet the individual appropriation of what is offered or mediated through the system *may* lead to a rejection or criticism of the organisation of the system – particularly if it leads, with impeccable internal logic, to the setting-up of inquisitions. The problem for the authorities or operators of a strong religious system is that the individuality – say, the individual's conscience – while in one sense being the point of the system, cannot be allowed to destroy the system, or even, too seriously, to disrupt the system, since otherwise the simplest form of continuity is threatened; and the importance of continuity for participants in a religious system is not because continuity is an end in itself, but because of a hope that other and future lives may have the opportunity of being similarly informed from the resources which are believed in all systems (with very different identifications of content) to be 'the words of life'. Thus in virtually all religious systems, and certainly in Christianity, there is an emphasis that it may be necessary to die in order to live, to lose one's self in order to find it, and *not* in fact to set up targets and goals, and 'strive officiously' to reach them. Not surprisingly this may well lead to serious conflicts between the individual appropri-ations of what is mediated through the system, and what the operators of a system believe is required for the successful continuity of the system.

Here is the real challenge to corporate believing. What sort of priority and status must be given to the means of a system's continuity, and how much divergence and individual creativity can the system encourage and tolerate, particularly when or if that individuality seems to be disruptive of the system? For the paradox is that while the systems *enable* us to be human (we are all born in particular cultures and

languages and belief systems), it is often the aberrant individual who turns back on a system which has given him life
and breathes new life into the system. Thus, while sometimes
the individual turns against the system and from that tension
a new system is eventually derived (Jesus and Jerusalem,
Luther and Rome, Gautama and Benares), it is not always
so: it is often the individual appropriation which justifies the
system by exhibiting, in the transformation of life, the truths
and possibilities towards which the system points, and for
which, at least in part, it exists.

And there is a further paradox: sensitive as we are to what
we take to be the oppressive nature of systems (restricting
individual liberty and curtailing freedom of expression), we
sometimes overlook the extent to which systems *enable*
creativity and freedom. In a strongly bounded system where
individuals know where they are and what counts as appropriate or inappropriate behaviour, they can get on with the
business of living without being preoccupied with the foundation of what they are doing. It is in this way that strongly
bounded systems may produce not only mindless conformity
(which sometimes happens) but, at the other extreme,
powerful and creative explorations of the implications of the
system in art, music, iconography, architecture, self-sac-
rificing lives and the like.

These themes of creative, though potentially and sometimes
actually oppressive, interactions between the individual and
the system have been explored, with reference to examples in
the history of art, in my article 'Art, Theology and Religious
Systems: A Case for the Inquisition?'[17] The same point can
be seen in Stravinsky's plea on behalf of dogma and for
the acceptance of the constraint of discipline as necessary
conditions of musical creativity – what he called 'the necessity
for order and discipline'.[18] In the passage which recalls what
was said earlier about the positive and liberating nature of
constraint (see note 7). Stravinsky wrote:

> As for myself, I experience a sort of terror when, at the
> moment of setting to work and finding myself before the
> infinitude of possibilities that present themselves, I have the
> feeling that everything is permissible to me; if everything is
> permissible to me, the best and the worst, if nothing offers

me any resistance, then any effort is inconceivable, and I cannot use anything as a basis, and consequently every undertaking becomes futile . . . So here we are, whether we like it or not, in the realm of necessity. And yet which of us has ever heard talk of art as other than a realm of freedom? This sort of heresy is uniformly widespread because it is imagined that art is outside the bounds of ordinary activity. Well, in art as in everything else, one can only build upon a resisting foundation . . . My freedom thus consists in my moving about within the narrow frame that I have assigned myself for each one of my undertakings.

I shall go even further: my freedom will be so much the greater and more meaningful the more narrowly I limit my field of action and the more I surround myself with obstacles. Whatever diminishes constraint, diminishes strength. The more constraints one imposes, the more one frees one's self of the chains that shackle the spirit.

. . . From all this we shall conclude the necessity of dogmatising on pain of missing our goal. If these words annoy and seem harsh, we can abstain from pronouncing them. For all that, they none the less contain the secret of salvation.[19]

No doubt there are others who would give a very different account of creativity, and who would insist that it depends on repudiation of tradition – on doing one's own thing. In the case of religious creativity, at the furthest extreme individuals will emerge who insist that true wisdom or insight or salvation or enlightenment, or whatever is held to be the ultimate goal, *cannot* be attained within or from any system. Thus, the *paribbajakas*, before and at the time of the Buddha, were known as *svayambhu*, the 'self-become', who attained enlightenment by their own effort, in independence from each other and everyone else. Furthermore they refused to teach anyone else, because such teaching would contradict the very way by which they had attained enlightenment. Martin Wiltshire has then applied this to the Buddha's own enlightenment and to his Great Hesitation after it, when he determined not to teach or instruct anybody else:

The fact that the Buddha hesitated to teach tells us something very important about the nature of Buddhist truth. He was not postulating the existence of a transcendent truth, about which one could formulate certain definite propositions to which one gives credence. He was postulating the existence of *immanent* truth (or, rather, that truth is immanent). This truth had no transcendent reference except *the way (magga)* to its realisation. Therefore, there is a very significant sense in which the Buddha found it difficult to teach the *dhamma* because there was no *content* to the enlightenment. That is not the same as saying there was no authentic experience of enlightenment, but simply that it could not be transmitted by set dogma or doctrine.[29]

Yet for all that, the Buddha recognised that cues of information, or of input, may be necessary to initiate the process towards enlightenment (indeed he received them himself), and that the continuity of the information process, however much it repudiates 'the closed fist of the teacher', requires formalisation. Thus the Sangha (the community of Buddhist monks), which is attributed in the canon to the Buddha's initiative and command, is a highly formal religious sub-system.

It may be that we are talking simply of the means that lead towards the end. But however true that may be, the means themselves are not equal; and since, for almost all of us, some means are necessary, and since therefore corporate believing is the condition in which we are bound to be if Christians, it is incumbent upon us to take extreme care in monitoring the nature of the system, or sub-system, in which and from which our lives are enabled – or in other words, to watch carefully that the system is *enabling* and not destructive of life in the Spirit: 'Though for no other cause, yet for this; that posterity may know we have not loosely through silence permitted things to pass away as in a dream, there shall be for men's information extant thus much concerning the present state of the Church of God established amongst us, and their careful endeavour which would have upheld the same.'

So opens the preface to Hooker's *Of the Laws of Ecclesiastical Polity*.[21] Hooker, in dealing with issues of authority, had to find a way between one extreme of systems maintenance and decision-making (in the individual conscience directly inspired, or in *sola scriptura*) and the other extreme (of a papal exercise of authority which was itself unbounded and uncontrolled): 'The disposition of these things resteth not now in the hands of popes, who live in no worldly awe or subjection, but is committed to them whom law may at all times bridle, and superior power control'; but conversely:

> If in so great variety of ways as the wit of man is easily able to find out towards any purpose, and in so great liking as all men especially have unto those inventions whereby some one shall seem to have been more enlightened from above than many thousands, the Church did give every man licence to follow what himself imagineth that 'God's Spirit doth reveal' unto him, or what he supposeth that God is likely to have revealed to some special person whose virtues deserve to be highly esteemed: what other effect could hereupon ensue, but the utter confusion of his Church under pretence of being taught, led and guided by his Spirit?

I doubt if we would wish to establish Hooker's ecclesiastical polity now, as he envisaged it then. But we should nevertheless be profoundly grateful that at least *one* sub-system within Christianity as a whole found, or was guided into, a middle way in the balance between the necessities for the system to mark its boundaries and to continue itself in time, and the freedom of individuals to appropriate what is offered in and through the system in very varied ways. Anglicanism is a constant source of amazed incredulity and unbelievable impossibility, as much to the insider as to the outside observer; and it has its own share of wicked abuse of the necessity for systems to be systems. Yet for all that, the Anglican settlement was a brilliant and extraordinary achievement, in securing a mutually creative balance between the system and the individual. To whom much has been given, much in the way of responsibility accrues.

The balance, then, between the system and the individual can be creative, just as also it can easily be abused. A clearer understanding of the necessities inherent in the process of information through time helps us to monitor more sensitively the nature of that interaction, and the disturbance which individual appropriation *may* cause in the system as a whole. If we know and understand more clearly what is going on, then we are perhaps more likely to retain *within* the system those 'disturbances' – those 'family rows'; and we may, too, gain wiser discrimination and greater courage in allowing them to become a creative enhancement of the system itself – of what the system maintains as the possibility and the purpose of life. Again, if we understand the necessary conditions of a system's continuity (or at least what a particular system identifies as the necessary conditions of its continuity), then we will be in a more independent position to be able to engage the issue of how different systems can be related to each other – different religions, for example, or different parts of the Christian Church.

Perhaps also it will remind us that if systems are necessary (as they are) to make possible the creative freedom of those who derive inspiration, truth and energy from them, we in turn have a *great* responsibility to sustain and nourish those whose work it is to maintain the system – the secretaries, the bishops, the stokers of boilers, the equivalent of the civil servants. Above all, in England, it would be the greatest possible folly if we do not give the highest priority and support to the parish – to the parochial clergy and lay people – where the system and its goals take on a living 'flesh and blood', and on which so much else depends.

Precisely for that reason, this reflection on the nature of religions as systems warns us to be on our guard against institutional imperialism. To allude briefly to an example: the Church in England has moved in recent years to increasing centralisation – for perfectly sensible and necessary reasons. But the exercise of that centralised management, in such manifestations as the implementation of the Sheffield Report (in itself a judicious survey), has evoked, from those on the receiving end, impotent cries of frustration and dismay, of which 'brutally stupid' seems to be one of the milder forms. Perhaps those reactions are ill grounded and misinformed. But confidence in a system, which is a decisive part of its efficacy, requires that perceptions (however ill informed) be taken very seriously indeed. It is even harder for the control figures in a system to conceive that they might be wrong

(because of the diffusion which occurs in collective responsibility) than it is for individuals.

Finally, it is important to remember how easily and quickly
a system can disintegrate if it removes, or allows to lapse, its
boundary-markers and its means of maintaining decision,
control and communication within the system and its
constituent parts. When control becomes oppressive it is not
surprising that the protest on behalf of the individual becomes
strong – and that *in itself* is a control mechanism, an answer
to the question: *Quis custodiet ipsos custodes?* – who keep an eye
on Big Brother when Big Brother is keeping an eye (and a
heavy foot) on us? Yet still the fact remains that the Church
as the recipient and the resource of grace *cannot* be casual
about the organised means through which it offers grace, life
and salvation to lives and generations beyond its own. The
Spirit indeed 'bloweth where it listeth'; but we cannot deduce
from *that* that the Spirit ignores the constraints of information
process in a universe of this sort, any more than we can
suppose that the incarnation circumvents the constraints of
humanity.[22]

The systematic nature of systems is undoubtedly open to
abuse and exploitation. All too easily the system becomes the
end in itself, instead of the means towards an End which lies
beyond itself. The responsibility of all Christians, in any
generation, is to transform – or to allow God to transform
through them – the dry bones of the system into a living
presence which in turn touches, heals, restores, sustains many
lives far beyond its own – much as W. F. Stead described it,
in miniature, in his poem *Festival in Tuscany:*

And down the lane a bellman came
Ringing a warning bell;
Then pipes were out and heads were bared,
A grave silence fell . . .

Black-gowned the wives and mothers walked,
Stark-faced and harrow-lined;
Under a darkly kerchiefed brow
Their eyes were wise and kind.

Behind them sons and fathers came,
With heavy step they trod;

Earth-stained and dumb with candles lit
And after them came God.

Christ on the Cross! thorns on His brow!
The spear-wounds in His side;
He poured His life into their lives
When He was crucified.

The Priest came bearing the sacred Host
Wherein Christ lives again:
We were but heathen, yet we kneeled
While God went down the lane.

The connection that needs to be carefully monitored is the one
that ensures the continuing *availability* of Christian resources
without being too dictatorial about the forms of their appropriation. This connection was handled with brilliant and
intuitive skill in the Anglican settlement through and after
the Reformation. Whether it is being, or can be, handled with
the same skill at the present time is one reason why the
Doctrine Commission was asked to attend to the subject of
corporate believing: 'For as in one body we have many
members, and all the members do not have the same function,
so we, though many, are one body in Christ, and individually
members one of another' (Rom: 12:4–5).

Notes

Preface

1. cf. Also the definition of Ambrose Bierce, *The Devil's Dictionary*, 'Faith, n. Belief without evidence in what is told by one who speaks without knowledge, of things without parallel' (*ed. cit.* p. 121).
2. The origin of this phrase is explained on p. 1.
3. The theme occurs as the assumption of the entire book; the sentence, 'Realism is long dead and gone' is on p. 245.
4. E. Dickinson, No. 1634, p. 671.
5. C. Kramarae, p. 28.

Chapter 1. The Burning Fuse

1. J. Bowker, 1983, p. 9.
2. 'Only connect . . .', *Christian*, vii, (1982), p. 66.
3. The point is summarised in R. Rucker, pp. 4–9. In a letter to *The Times*, November 1976, the socialist Ben Vincent exemplified the derogatory sense: 'Sir, There appear to be no other socialists who read *The Times*. . . . Can you not see, any of you, that some day your descendants will be grateful for the abolition of a system of class conflict and competition . . . ? At least such an ideal should surely be discussed now and then, and not totally excluded from your pages as if it were the merest academic theology.'
4. *Daily Telegraph*, 9 May 1979, p. 1.
5. ibid, p. 11.
6. Ironically, there is one religion which does have a discussion of, not exactly how many angels can stand on the head of a pin, but how many *deva-s* (shining heavenly beings) can stand on the tip of a hair. That religion is Buddhism. The irony lies in the fact that Buddhism is often proclaimed in the West as

a non-theistic philosophy or way of life; and it is often stated that it is not a religion. Buddhism is both theistic (with its own understanding of what theistic appearances are and are not: see my *Religious Imagination*, pp. 244–307) and a religion. The discussion of 'how many *deva-s* on the tip of hair' occurs because of the description of the death of the Buddha in the Mahaparinibbana Sutta (2.139), during which *deva-s* crowded around, as many as can balance on the thickness of a hair. Later commentators (e.g. Buddhaghosa) claimed that 20 to 60 could stand on the pin-prick of a needle without disturbing each other.

7. S. Smith, p. 308.
8. A. Huxley, pp. 270f.
9. The sentence was used by Harold Wilson at the Labour Party Conference of that year, in Scarborough. It is more often cited with 'technological' substituted for 'scientific'.
10. Quoted from M. B. Strauss, p. 247.
11. 'If way to the Better there be, it exacts a full look at the worst', *In Tenebris*.
12. 'Say Not the Struggle Naught Availeth.'
13. H. Thoreau, p. 321.
14. ibid.
15. John of Salisbury, p. 131.
16. Greek mystery religions are a familiar example, as, in the East, are Hindu and Buddhist tantric cults. For a precise example of this point (in the way in which early rabbinic Judaism designated its orally-transmitted *mishnah* as its own *misteyrin* – because Christians could not get access to it as they could to publicly available Scripture), see my article, 'Mystery and Parable'.
17. J. Bowker, *Worlds of Faith*, p. 213.
18. See Bowker, 'Religions as Systems', in *Believing in the Church*, pp. 159–89.
19. ibid, p. 167.
20. These points are argued and illustrated at length in my forthcoming book, *Dying and Disorder: Secular and Religious Understandings of Death*.
21. Following Kuhn and Feyerabend (see pp. 51–3 of this book), there has been an immense discussion of theory displacement and incommensurability, from which it is clear that there is no smooth process whereby what is of value in T(heory)[1] is accumulated in T[2] as T[2] subsumes T[1], while whatever is erroneous is discarded. For a brief summary, see I. Hacking, pp. 65–74.

22. Theory-displacement is even more complicated in the case of religions, but scarcely any applied research in this field has been undertaken.
23. The Five Precepts are the basic obligations which a Buddhist promises to himself to undertake. See Bowker, *Worlds of Faith*, p. 28.
24. This forms vol. xxvi, No. 1 (1984), *Race and Class: A Journal for Black and Third World Liberation*. There is a wider survey of some of these issues in T. Ling, 1979.
25. This is the opening scene of Tolstoy's *Anna Karenina*.
26. In H. A. Jack, p. 6.
27. J. Bowker, *Worlds of Faith*, p. 293.
28. M. Daly, p. 39.
29. This is particularly evident in the interviews with women in *Worlds of Faith*. See especially pp. 210ff.
30. Quoted from K. Tsurumi, p. 167.
31. ibid. pp. 138ff.
32. e.g. my article, 'Can Differences Make a Difference?'
33. See *Worlds of Faith*, pp. 34f.
34. This is again particularly clear in *Worlds of Faith*, where many more than half the people we interviewed were refugees from persecution; see, e.g. pp. 20ff.
35. This is the title of his autobiographical account of his discovery of India and of its consequence for his Christian vocation.
36. An account of the trials appeared in *The Times*, June 1981, under the headline, 'Delhi Court Says Gods Can Smoke'.

Chapter 2. Is There Anybody There?

1. *Hamlet* i.v. 16ff.
2. Bowker, *Worlds of Faith*, p. 10.
3. 1 John 4: 12 (AV).
4. For an account of this and its implications for Blake, see H. N. Fairchild, pp. 71–3.
5. G. Bottomley, 'Second Interlude', in *Festival Preludes*.
6. R. Skelton, p. 127.
7. D. Cupitt, 1980, p. 56.
8. A. Huxley, p. 24.
9. T. Stoppard, p. 75. In point of fact, 'special relativity is very much concerned with what is invariant and so reliable. It points to interval rather than distance as fulfilling that role. Einstein would have hated a chaotic relativism' (J. Polkinghorne, personal communication).

10. Cupitt, 1984, p. 31.
11. ibid, p. 263.
12. C. Webb, p. 422.
13. D. MacKay, p. 1.
14. Cupitt, op. cit. p. 265.
15. B. Barnes, in ed. M. Hollis, p. 23.
16. ibid. p. 28.
17. An effective summary of the positions briefly alluded to is contained in R. Rorty, *The Mirror of Nature*.
18. Cupitt, op. cit. p. 11.
19. The extent and consequences of this endeavour are discussed briefly in my *The Sense of God*, and also, in more detail, in 'The Aeolian Harp: Sociobiology and Human Judgement'.
20. E. Renan, *L'Avenir de la Science*, 1848, quoted from Stromberg, pp. 26f.
21. See p. 46.
22. Quoted from Stromberg, p. 25.
23. J. Tyndall, II, p. 197.
24. T. H. Huxley, I, p. 333.
25. Kelvin, p. 486.
26. ibid. p. 492.
27. ibid.
28. O. R. Frisch, p. 39.
29. ibid. p. 527.
30. Planck was himself (obviously from a chronological point of view) educated within the framework of the Newtonian ambition. When he embarked on his research, he was (according to his own account) warned by Professor Jolly that physics was 'an almost fully mature science . . . Perhaps one could find in a corner, or in a niche, a spot of dust or a little bubble worth examining, but the system was well established.' But his own statement (when he received the Nobel prize) indicates how deep the divergence was: 'It revealed something absolutely new, something upheard of, which seemed destined to revolutionise our ideas of physics which, since the foundation of the differential calculus by Leibniz and Newton, were based upon the assumption of the continuity of all causal relations' (see W. Ehrenberg, p. 57).
31. The point (albeit familiar) is summarised by I. Prigogine (pp. 214f.): 'The basis of the vision of classical physics was the conviction that the future is determined by the present, and therefore a careful study of the present permits the unveiling of the future. At no time, however, was this more than a theoretical possibility. Yet in some sense this unlimited

predictability was an essential element of the scientific picture of the physical world. We may perhaps even call it the founding myth of classical science.

'The situation is greatly changed today. It is remarkable that this change results basically from our better understanding of the limitations of measurement processes because of the necessity to take into account the role of the observer . . . The incorporation of the limitation of our way of acting on nature has been an essential element of progress.

'The role of the observer in quantum mechanics has been a recurrent theme in the scientific literature in the past fifty years. Whatever the future developments are, this role is essential. The naive realism of classical physics, which assumed that properties of matter were "there" independently of the experimental device, had to be revised.'

32. F. Dyson, pp. 248f; though in fact not all physicists *would* agree with quite so strong a statement.
33. J. Gribbin, p. 2.
34. Davis and Hersh, p. 410.
35. ibid.
36. In *The Times Literary Supplement*, 29 October, 1982, p. 1198.
37. T. Kuhn, p. 171.
38. P. Feyerabend, pp. 189.
39. This is the title of his book (see Bibliography), in which he states the contrast in this way: 'There is a tendency to think of nineteenth-century painting in terms of Realism, Positivism and "establishment" art . . . The other side of the picture, while it was influenced by these stages in the history of art, ran more or less directly counter to them. Often governed by that queen of all the faculties, the imagination, this alternative tradition drew its eleoquence from the individual's power of expression, whether in silence or in impassioned utterance, in dream or in waking clarity. Goya with his extravagance was a contemporary of Louis David; the visions of Blake date from the same period as Canova's marbles' (p. 7.)
40. Quoted from H. B. Chipp, p. 48.
41. L. Nochlin, p. 142.
42. Quoted from ibid. p. 144.
43. 'Naturalism in the Salon', quoted from R. N. Stromberg, pp. 157. 154.
44. V. van Gogh, p. 107.
45. In R. Friedenthal, II, p. 256.
46. Illustrated in ibid. p. 257 (though the lithographs are considerably later in date, 1945/6.

47. Carl André, Equivalent VIII.
48. N. Goodman (1978), title of ch. 4.
49. ibid. p. 19. It should be noted that Goodman continues in a critically realist direction: 'Nevertheless, showing or exemplifying, like denoting, is a referential function; and much the same considerations count for pictures as for the concepts or predicates of a theory: their relevance and their revelations, their force and their fit – in sum their *rightness*.'
50. N. Goodman (1976), pp. 92f.
51. P. Griffiths, pp. 127f.
52. D. Mitchell, p. 77 (though the collusion could scarcely have been literal, since the painting was not on public view for many years after).
53. J. Golding, p. 47.
54. D. Mitchell, p. 85f., quoting E. Stein, *Orpheus in New Guises*, p. 51.
55. ibid. p. 91.
56. Ibid.
57. W. Tucker, p. 107.
58. The formula is that of B. Lonergan, who exposes in his book, *Insight*, the poverty of the view that 'what is obvious in knowing, is what knowing obviously is'.
59. B. Magee, p. 107.
60. Thus Magee continued: 'So a former Logical Positivist such as yourself, although you now say that most of the doctrines were false, still adopts the same general approach; and you are still addressing yourself to very much the same questions, though in a more liberal, open way?' To which Ayer replied, 'I would say so, yes' (p. 108).
61. M. Bunge, p. 61. cf. Peter Kapitza's variation on Anita Loos. ('Kissing your hand may make you feel very good, but a diamond and sapphire bracelet lasts for ever'): 'Theory is a good thing, but a good experiment lasts for ever.'
62. M. Devitt, p. 3. Realism, in Devitt's understanding 'is an overarching ontological doctrine about what there is and what it's like. It is committed to most of the physical points of common sense and science, and to the view that these entities are independent of the mental. It has an epistemic aspect: the entities do not depend for their existence or nature on our opinion; they exist objectively . . .

   'Any doctrine of truth is a semantic doctrine. It may see truth as ascriptively redundant; a disquotational notion. If it does not – if it sees truth as explanatory – it must find a place for truth in the theory of people (believer-desirers). So its place is in a theory of a small, but important, part of the world the Realist believes in' (p. 227).

63. W. Quine, p. 295.
64. F. Suppe, p. 618.
65. B. Barnes, p. 2.
66. ibid. pp. 18, 24.
67. ibid. p. 2.
68. N. Jardine, p. 23.
69. ibid. p. 37.
70. ibid. p. 40.
71. ibid. p. 25.
72. B. Barnes, op. cit. pp. 25f.
73. The pharase is the title of his book, and also half the title of one of the essays in it, which begins with a quotation from Whitman's *Specimen Days*, which anticipates the point: 'The most profound theme that can occupy the mind of man – the problem on whose solution science, art, the bases and pursuits of nations, and everything else, including intelligent human happiness (here today, 1882, New York, Texas, California, the same as all times, all lands) . . . is doubtless involved in the query: what is the fusing explanation and tie – what the relation between the (radical, democratic) Me, the human identity of understanding, emotions, spirit, etc., on the one side, of and with the (conservative) Not Me, the whole of the material objective universe and laws, with what is behind them in time and space, on the other side?'
74. The point was made by Einstein himself, in his 'letter to Newton', in his *Autobiographical Notes*. Having emphasised the contrast between their views, Einstein pulled himself up: 'Enough of this. Newton forgive me. You found the only way that, in your day, was at all possible for a man of the highest powers of intellect and creativity. The concepts that you created still dominate the way we think in physics, although we now know that they must be replaced by others farther removed from the sphere of immediate experience if we want to try for a more profound understanding of the way things are interrelated.'
75. For this account see A. B. Fraser, p. 102.
76. A. Quinton, p. 182.
77. There is an introductory account of Husserl in the final chapter of my *The Sense of God*.
78. R. S. Tragesser, pp. 18f.
79. Quoted from J. Calado, reviewing M. Goldman, *The Demon in the Aether. TLS*, 20 April 1984, p. 442.

80. S. Johnson, I, p. 111: 'What Baudius says of Erasmus seems applicable to him (Milton), *magis habuit quod fugeret, quod sequeretur*. He had determined rather what to condemn, than what to approve . . . We know rather what he was not than what he was.'
81. G. M. Hopkins, p. 90.
82. S. Plath, 'Black Rook in Rainy Weather':

> A certain minor light may still
> Leap incandescent
> Out of a kitchen table or chair
> As if a celestial burning took
> Possession of the most obtuse objects now and then –
> Thus hallowing an interval
> Otherwise inconsequent
> By bestowing largesse, honour,
> One might say love. At any rate, I now walk
> Wary (for it could happen
> Even in thus dull, ruinous landscape); sceptical,
> Yet politic; ignorant
> Of whatever angel may choose to flare
> Suddenly at my elbow. I only know that a rook
> Ordering its black feathers can so shine
> As to seize my senses, haul
> My eyelids up, and grant
> A brief respite from fear
> Of total neutrality.

83. T. Stoppard, p. 71.

Chapter 3. Why Believe in God?

1. Quoted from W. S. Smith.
2. M. Gardner, p. 283.
3. See A. J. Morin, pp. 295f.
4. *Hist.*, vi. 56.
5. K. Marx, Introduction to 'Contribution to the Critique of Hegel's Philosophy of Right'.
6. For accounts of this, and for an example of its application to ritual, see Bibliography, E. G. d'Aquili.
7. See esp. pp. 185f.
8. Quoted in Bowker, 1983 (*Zygon*), p. 356; the editorial Introduction is a summary of these issues.
9. E. O. Wilson, p. 192.

10. There is a discussion of this point in my *The Sense of God*, ch. 7, 'The Physiology of the Brain and Claims to Religious Experience'.
11. Bowker, 1983, pp. 154f.
12. E. Dickinson, No. 510, pp. 248f.
13. J. Mortimer, p. 44.
14. W. de la Mare, pp. xxxivf.
15. R. Swinburne, p. 277, 291.
16. B. Russell, p. 845.
17. D. Cupitt, 1984, p. 271.
18. Quoted from Kenin and Wintle, *ad loc.*
19. Quoted from N. Rees, p. 192.
20. The form of the fallacy frequently appears in titles or chapter headings. For example, in N. H. Brasher: 'Peel and the Tories, Martyr or Renegade? Palmerston and Foreign Policy, Ginger Beer or Champagne? Gladstone, Statesman or Bigot? Disraeli, Statesman or Charlatan? Joseph Chamberlain, Egoist or Visionary?'
21. W. R. Ashby, p. 3; the sentence and its implications are more fully discussed in my *The Sense of God*, p. 88.
22. Although the conclusion is a commonplace of theological reflection, this particular sentence occurs as the motto on the self-portrait of Salvatore Rosa in the National Gallery.
23. The transcript of this discussion, 'Genes, Mind and Culture', has been published in *Zygon*, xix (1984), pp. 213–32.
24. E. Dickinson, No. 76, pp. 39f.

Appendix: Religions as Systems

1. Bannock, 1971.
2. Frisch, 1964, pp. 3, 41.
3. G. MacGregor, 'No Living With or Without God', in G. Johnston and W. Roth, eds. *The Church in the Modern World* (Toronto, Ryerson), p. 15.
4. E. Muir, 'Soliloquy', in *Collected Poems 1921–1958*, pp. 196–7.
5. A. Tennyson, 'The Princess', iv, in *Early Poems* (1900), p. 306.
6. Bowker, 1978, p. 9.
7. In more technical language, religions offer various forms of *constraint*, which, if they are appropriated or internalised, delimit the life of an individual or group, and help to control it into its particular outcomes. The vital point to grasp is that although the notion of constraint sounds negative and restrictive (which initially it is) it is in fact extremely liberating

and creative. Without constraints no life (nor even a universe) is possible, because available energy would, so to speak, flow randomly in all directions (except, of course, that there could not *be* any direction without constraint), instead of being organised into planets or people. The paradox is that the more elaborate the constraints are, the greater the freedom there is for possible behaviours; or to put it, as Ashby does, in the context of cybernetics: 'When a constraint exists, advantage can usually be taken of it' (*An Introduction to Cybernetics*, p. 130). For a fuller discussion of these points, which are critical in understanding the positive nature of religions as systems, see my own books, *The Sense of God*, pp. 86ff. and *The Religious Imagination*, pp. 17ff.

8. New York, Random House 1979.
9. Cape 1979.
10. Barnes, 1980, pp. 66–7.
11. On 4 September 1975 the Unification Church applied to the New York State Supreme Court to be admitted to the New York Council of Churches, on the ground that it is 'a Christian Church committed to the ministry of spreading by word and deed, the gospel of the Divine Lord and Saviour Jesus Christ' (see *Occasional Bulletin*, i, 3 [1977], p. 18). However the National Council of the Churches of Christ in the USA then commissioned a study comparing the official doctrinal text of the Unification Church (*Divine Principle*) with Scripture; and that study concluded: 'The role and authority of Scripture are compromised in the teachings of the Unification Church; revelations are invoked as divine and normative in *Divine Principle* which contradict basic elements of Christian faith; a "new, ultimate, final truth" is presented to complete and supplant all previously recognized religious teachings, including those of Christianity.'
12. H. Rahn, *et al.*, 'How Bird Eggs Breathe', *Sci. Am.*, 240 (1979), p. 38.
13. Bobbitt, *et al.*, 1978, pp. 365ff.
14. Walker, 1968, p. 520.
15. For an introductory description, see von Campenhausen, 1969.
16. Phillipson, 1966, p. 34. 34.
17. *Zygon*, 13 (1978), pp. 313–32.
18. Stravinsky, 1977, pp. 61ff.
19. ibid. pp. 63–5.
20. From an entry in the forthcoming J. W. Bowker, ed. *Oxford Companion to Religions of the World*.

21. *The Works of that Learned and Judicious Divine, Mr Richard Hooker* (1885), p. 88 (Preface i.1).
22. In *The Religious Imagination* I have tried to show how these considerations of constraint and creativity can be applied historically to Jesus and how they lead to a thoroughgoing doctrine of incarnation.

Bibliography

Ashby, W. R., *An Introduction to Cybernetics*. London 1956.

Bannock, G., *The Juggernauts: The Age of the Big Corporation*. London, Weidenfeld 1971.

Barnes, B., *Interests and the Growth of Knowledge*. London, Routledge 1977.

Scientific Knowledge and Sociological Theory. London, Routledge 1980.

Bellak, L., M. Hurvich and H. K. Gediman, *Ego Functions in Schizophrenics, Neurotics, and Normals*. New York, Wiley 1973.

Bierce, A., *The Enlarged Devil's Dictionary*, ed. E. J. Hopkins, Harmondsworth, Penguin 1984.

Bobbitt, H. R., *et al.*, *Organizational Behaviour: Understanding and Prediction*. New Jersey, Prentice-Hall 1978.

Bottomley, G., *Poems of Twenty Years*, London 1938.

Bowker, J. W., *The Sense of God: Sociological, Anthropological, and Psychological Approaches to the Origin of the Sense of God*, Oxford University Press, 1973.

'Can Differences Make a Difference? A Comment on Tillich's Proposals for Dialogue Between Religions', *JTS* xxiv (1973), pp. 158–88.

'Mystery and Parable: Mark iv. 1–20', *JTS*, xxv (1974), pp. 300–17.

The Religious Imagination and the Sense of God, Oxford University Press 1978.

'The Aeolian Harp: Sociobiology and Human Judgement', *Zygon*, xv (1980), pp. 307–33.

Believing in the Church, Report of Doctrine Commission of the Church of England, ch. 6. SPCK 1981.

'Only Connect . . .', *Christian*, vii (1982), pp. 59–65.

Worlds of Faith: Religious belief and Practice in Britain Today, London, Ariel 1983.

ed., *Origins, Functions and Management of Aggression in Biocultural Evolution*, *Zygon*, xxiii (1983).

Brasher, N. H., *Arguments in History: Britain in the Nineteenth Century*. London, Macmillan 1968.

Bunge, M., 'What Are Physical Theories About?', in *Studies in the Philosophy of Science*, Am. Phil. Soc. Monograph Series, III (1969), pp. 61–99.

Chipp, H. B., *Theories of Modern Art: A Source Book by Artists And Critics*, Berkeley, California University Press 1968.

Cupitt, D., *Taking Leave of God*, London, SCM 1980.
The Sea of Faith: Christianity in Change. London, BBC 1984.

Daly, M., *Gyn/Ecology: The Meta-ethics of Radical Feminism*, London, The Women's Press 1979.

d'Aquili, E. G., and C. D. Laughlin, *Biogenetic Structuralism*, New York, Columbia University Press 1974.
The Spectrum of Ritual: A Biogenetic Structural Analysis, New York, Columbia University Press 1979.

Davis, P. J., and R. Hersh, *The Mathematical Experience*, London, Penguin 1983.

de la Mare, W., *Love*, London, Faber 1943.

Devitt, M., *Realism and Truth*, Oxford, Blackwell 1984.

Dickinson, E., *The Complete Poems*, London, Faber 1970.

Dyson, F., *Disturbing the Universe*, London, Pan 1981.

Ehrenberg, W., *Dice of the Gods: Causality, Necessity and Chance*, London, Birkbeck 1977.

Fairchild, H. N., *Religious Trends in English Poetry*, New York, Columbia University Press 1949.

Feyerabend, P., *Against Method: Towards an Anarchistic Theory of Knowledge*, London, New Left Books 1975.

Fraser, A. B., and W. H. Mach, 'Mirages', *Sci.Am.*, ccxxxiv (1976) pp. 102–11.

Friedenthal, R., *Letters of the Great Artists*, London, Thames and Hudson 1963.

Frisch, M., *Andorra*. London, Methuen 1964.

Frisch, O. R., *The Nature of Matter*. London, Thames and Hudson 1972.

Gardiner, M., *The Whys of a Philosophical Scrivener*, Brighton, Harvester 1983.

Gillispie, C. C., *The Edge of Objectivity: An Essay in the History of Scientific Ideas*, New Jersey, Princeton 1960.

Golding, J., *Cubism: A History and an Analysis, 1907–1914*, London, Faber 1968.

Goodman, N., *Languages of Art: An Approach to a Theory of Symbols*, Indianapolis, Hackett 1976.
Ways of Worldmaking, Sussex, Harvester 1978.

Gribbin, J., *In Search of Schrodinger's Cat*, London, Corgi 1985.

Griffiths, B., *The Marriage of East and West*, London, Collins 1982.

Griffiths, P., *A Concise History of Modern Music from Debussy to Boulez*, London, Thames and Hudson 1978.

Gunn, G., *The Interpretation of Otherness*, Oxford University Press 1979.

Hacking, I., *Representing and Intervening: Introductory Topics in the Philosophy of Natural Science*, Cambridge University Press 1983.

Hollis, M., and S. Lukes, *Rationality and Relativism*, Oxford, Blackwell 1982.

Hopkins, G. M., *The Poems*, Oxford University Press 1970.

Huxley, A., *Texts and Pretexts*, London, Chatto 1932.
Collected Essays, London, Chatto 1960.

Huxley, T. H., *The Life and Letters of Huxley*, London, Macmillan 1903.

Jack, H. A., ed., *Religion in the Struggle for World Community*, World Conference on Religion and Peace 1980.

Jardine, N., 'The Possibility of Absolutism', in ed. D. H. Mellor, *Science, Belief and Behaviour*, Cambridge University Press 1980.

John of Salisbury (ed. J. A. Giles), *Opera Omnia*, Oxford 1848.

Johnson, S., *Lives of the English Poets*, Oxford University Press 1906.

Kapitza, P., *Experiment, Theory, Practice*, Studies in the Philosophy of Science, xlvi, Boston 1980.

Kelvin, Lord, *Baltimore Lectures on Molecular Dynamics and the Wave Theory of Light*, Cambridge University Press 1904.

Kenin, R., and J. Wintle, *The Dictionary of Biographical Quotation*, New York, Knopf 1978.

Kramarae, C., and P. A. Treichler, *A Feminist Dictionary*, London, Pandora 1985.

Kuhn, T., *The Structure of Scientific Revolutions*, Chicago University Press 1962.

Ling, T., *Buddhism, Imperialism and War*, London, Allen and Unwin 1979.

Lonergan, B. F., *Insight*, New York Phil. Library 1970.

McGinley, P., *Times Three*, New York, Viking Pr. 1960 and London, Secker & Warburg 1961.

MacKay, D. M., 'Language, Meaning and God', *Philosophy*, xlvii (1972).

Magee, B., *Men of Ideas: Some Creators of Contemporary Philosophy*, Oxford University Press 1982.

Margulies, D. M., 'Selective Attention and the Brain: A Hypothesis Concerning the Hippocarpal-Ventral Striatal Axis, the Mediation of Selective Attention, and the Pathogenesis of Attentional Disorders', *Medical Hypotheses*, xviii (1985), pp. 221–64.

Mitchell, D., *The Language of Modern Music*, London, Faber 1966.

Morin, A. J., 'Sociobiology and Religion: Conciliation or Confrontation?', *Zygon*, xv (1980), pp. 295–306.

Mortimer, J., *A Voyage Round my Father*, London, Methuen 1971.

Muir, E., *Collected Poems 1921–1958*. London, Faber 1960.

Nochlin, L., *Realism*, Harmondsworth, Penguin 1971.

O'Keefe, M. L., *The Farthest Thunder: A Comparison of Emily Dickinson and St John of the Cross*, private pubn 1979.

Phillipson, J., *Ecological Energetics*, Lodnon, Arnold 1966.

Pirsig, R. M., *Zen and the Art of Motorcycle Maintenance: An Inquiry into Values*, London, Corgi 1976.

Prigogine, I., *From Being to Becoming: Time and Complexity in the Physical Sciences*, San Francisco, Freeman 1980.

Quine, W. V. O., 'Relativism and Absolutism', *The Monist*, lxvii, pp. 293–5.

Quinton, A., *The Nature of Things*, London, Routledge 1973.

Rees, N., *Sayings of the Century*, London, Alan Unwin 1984.

Roberts-Jones, P., *Beyond Time and Place: Non-Realist Painting in the Nineteenth Century*, Oxford University Press 1978.

Rorty, R., *Philosophy and the Mirror of Nature*, Oxford, Blackwell 1980.

Rucker, R., *Infinity and the Mind: The Science and Philosophy of the Infinite*, London, Paladin 1984.

Russell, B., *History of Western Philosophy* . . . London, Allen & Unwin 1954.

Skelton, R., *Poetic Truth*, London Heinemann 1978.

Smith, S., *Collected Poems*, London, Penguin 1982.

Smith, W. S., *Shaw on Religion*, London, Constable 1967.

'Sri Lanka: Racism, and the Authoritarian State', *Race and Class*, xxvi (1984).

Stein, E., *Orpheus in New Guises*, London, Rockliff 1953.

Stoppard, T., *Jumpers*, London, Faber 1972.

Strauss, M. B., *Familiar Medical Quotations*, Boston, Little, Brown 1968.

Stravinsky, I., *Poetics of Music in the Form of Six Lessons*, Cambridge, Mass., Harvard 1977.

Stromberg, R. N., *Realism, Naturalism and Symbolism*, New York, Harper 1968.

Suppe, F., *The Structure of Scientific Theories*, Illinois University Press 1977.

Swinburne, R., *The Existence of God*, Oxford University Press 1979.

Thoreau, H. D., *Walden*, New Jersey, Princeton 1971.

Tragasser, R. S., *Husserl and Realism in Logic and Mathematics*, Cambridge Univeristy Press 1984.

Tsurumi, K., *Social Change and the Individual: Japan Before and After Defeat in World War II*, New Jersey, Princeton 1970.

Tucker, W., *The Language of Sculpture*, London, Thames and Hudson 1977.

Tyndall, J., *Fragments of Science*, London 1889.

van Gogh, V., *Letters to an Artist: From Vincent van Gogh to Anton Ridder van Rappard, 1881–85*, London, Constable 1936.

von Campenhausen, H., *Ecclesiastical Authority and Spiritual Power in the Church of the First Three Centuries*, London, Black 1969.

Walker, B., *Hindu World*, London, Allen & Unwin 1968.

Webb, C. C. J., 'On Some Recent Movements in Philosophy . . .', in *Transactions of the Third Intnl Congress for the History of Religions*, ii (Oxford, 1908), pp. 416–24.

Wigner, E., 'The Unreasonable Effectiveness of Mathematics in the Natural Sciences', *Communications on Pure and Applied Mathematics*, xiii (1960).

Wiles, M., ed., *Christian Believing*, London, SPCK 1976.

Wilson, E. O., *On Human Nature*, Cambridge, Mass., Harvard 1978.

Index

Index of Names